P9-CEO-989

Finance and Capital Markets

NATIONAL BUREAU OF ECONOMIC RESEARCH
General Series 96

Economic Research: Retrospect and Prospect

FINANCE AND CAPITAL MARKETS

Fiftieth Anniversary Colloquium II

NATIONAL BUREAU OF ECONOMIC RESEARCH
NEW YORK 1972

Distributed by COLUMBIA UNIVERSITY PRESS
NEW YORK AND LONDON

Library of Congress card number: 71-187317
ISBN: 0-87014-252-6 (hard cover)
ISBN: 0-87014-277-1 (paperback)
Printed in the United States of America

Relation of National Bureau Directors to Publications
Reporting Proceedings of the Fiftieth Anniversary Colloquia

Since the present volume is a record of colloquium proceedings, it has been exempted from the rules governing submission of manuscripts to, and critical review by, the Board of Directors of the National Bureau.

(*Resolution adopted July 6, 1948, as revised November 21, 1949, and April 20, 1968*)

Prefatory Note

This volume of the Fiftieth Anniversary Series contains the proceedings of Finance and Capital Markets, a colloquium held in New York City on October 22, 1970. We are indebted to Raymond W. Goldsmith and to those members of the Bureau's Board of Directors who served on the committee to plan and coordinate the session: Tom E. Davis, Albert J. Hettinger, Maurice W. Lee, J. Wilson Newman, James J. O'Leary, George B. Roberts, Robert V. Roosa, George Cline Smith, Willis J. Winn and Donald B. Woodward. We are also grateful to Gnomi Gouldin, Virginia Meltzer, Ester Moskowitz, and Ruth Ridler, who prepared the manuscript for publication.

ROBERT E. LIPSEY

Fiftieth Anniversary Colloquium Series

To commemorate its fiftieth anniversary the National Bureau of Economic Research sponsored a series of colloquia to explore the effects of pending and anticipated policy issues on future research priorities for areas of long-standing Bureau concern. As a basis for the panel and audience discussions, economists specializing in the subject area prepared papers in which they reviewed relevant research advances through time and presented their opinions for the direction of future effort. These papers, and in some instances edited transcripts of panelists' comments, appear as part of the National Bureau's Fiftieth Anniversary publications series. Papers developed for the colloquia and publications series and participants in the program included:

THE BUSINESS CYCLE TODAY

September 24, 1970—New York City

Moderators:

Morning session: Paul A. Samuelson
Afternoon session: F. Thomas Juster

Presentations:

"Dating American Growth Cycles" *Ilse Mintz*
"The 'Recession' of 1969–1970" *Solomon Fabricant*
"The Cyclical Behavior of Prices" *Geoffrey H. Moore*
"Forecasting Economic Conditions: The Record and the Prospect" *Victor Zarnowitz*
"Econometric Model Simulations and the Cyclical Characteristics of the U.S. Economy" *Victor Zarnowitz*
"A Study of Discretionary and Nondiscretionary Monetary and Fiscal Policies in the Context of Stochastic Macroeconometric Models" *Yoel Haitovsky and Neil Wallace*

Panelists:

Morning session: Otto Eckstein, Henry C. Wallich
Afternoon session: Bert G. Hickman, Arthur M. Okun

FINANCE AND CAPITAL MARKETS
October 22, 1970—New York City

Moderator: Robert V. Roosa

Presentation:

"Finance and Capital Markets" *John Lintner*

Panelists: William J. Baumol, Sidney Homer, James J. O'Leary

A ROUNDTABLE ON POLICY ISSUES AND RESEARCH OPPORTUNITIES IN INDUSTRIAL ORGANIZATION
November 5, 1970—Chicago, Illinois

Moderator: Victor R. Fuchs

Presentations:

"Industrial Organization: Boxing the Compass" *James W. McKie*
"Antitrust Enforcement and the Modern Corporation" *Oliver E. Williamson*
"Issues in the Study of Industrial Organization in a Regime of Rapid Technical Change" *Richard R. Nelson*
"Industrial Organization: A Proposal for Research" *Ronald H. Coase*

PUBLIC EXPENDITURES AND TAXATION

December 2, 1970—Washington, D.C.

Moderator: Walter W. Heller

Presentation:

"Quantitative Research in Taxation and Government Expenditure"

Carl S. Shoup

Panelists: James M. Buchanan, Richard R. Musgrave

ECONOMIC GROWTH

December 10, 1970—San Francisco, California

Moderator: R. Aaron Gordon

Presentation:

"Is Growth Obsolete?"

William D. Nordhaus and James Tobin

Panelists: Moses Abramovitz, Robin C. O. Matthews

HUMAN RESOURCES

May 13, 1971—Atlanta, Georgia

Moderator: Gary S. Becker

Presentation:

"Human Capital: Policy Issues and Research Opportunities"

Theodore W. Schultz

Panelists: Alice M. Rivlin, Gerald S. Somers

THE FUTURE OF ECONOMIC RESEARCH

April 23, 1971—South Brookline, Massachusetts

Presentation:

"Quantitative Economic Research: Trends and Problems"

Simon Kuznets

Contents

Foreword

The study of finance and capital markets was a comparatively late starter among the fields that occupied the National Bureau over its first fifty years. However, as John Lintner's careful and thorough survey shows, the Bureau's studies in these areas, beginning in the late 1930's with the assistance of a series of exploratory committees, provided a wide variety of new knowledge where information had been extremely scarce. The Bureau's contribution was of two types. One was the establishment of comprehensive frameworks of accounts which were intended to be of service in studying many different questions about the whole economy or the interrelationships among sectors. Each of these studies (for example, those of the flow of funds, the stock of tangible wealth, and national and sectoral balance sheets) not only collected or organized a wide variety of data but also weighed conceptual problems and established a set of methods for later use, by the Bureau or by others such as government agencies who carried on the effort. These studies were in the tradition of the earlier work on the concepts and measurement of national income, which had gone so far in establishing the Bureau's role and reputation. The second type of study, especially those that were part of the Financial Research Program, consisted of the detailed examination of particular financial instruments and institutions, filling gaps in information and replacing casual impressions with quantitative knowledge.

An institution such as the National Bureau, whose mission is a public one, must regularly reexamine its research priorities. Some of the basic research projects which Lintner describes as the chief ornaments of the Bureau's contribution to the study of finance must have seemed distressingly long-range in their objectives, considered against the background of the urgent current problems of the 1930's, 1940's, and 1950's, when they were inaugurated. Yet, as Lintner reviews this record, it seems evident that some of the immediately least relevant projects have since had the widest benefits. These benefits have come not only from the particular publications but from the stimulus to others, in the National Bureau as well as outside, in government and other research organizations. And the stimulus has spread in widening circles to produce improvements both in data and in theoretical analysis, even though the original theoretical bases for some of the work, as Lintner points out, now seem primitive or have been superseded by later efforts.

That record of achievement has usually influenced the Bureau's choice of studies in favor of basic research, often involving the collection or organization of large quantities of new data. In looking toward the future, however, Lintner and the discussants of his paper seem to agree on the desirability of some redirection of effort away from the major data gathering programs, which have been a large part of the Bureau's research program in finance. They urge greater attention to analytical studies of financial markets, using theoretical developments which have occurred since the time most of the Bureau's research in this area was done.

It is a pleasure to be able to report that, as if in anticipation of the recommendations, some progress has already been made in at least two of the areas suggested for future study. One of these is the disaggregation of the residual or household sector in balance sheet and flow-of-funds accounts and another is the examination of the effect of inflation on financial markets.

On the first question, a small step was taken with the National Bureau's report to the Securities and Exchange Commission on institutional investment and the market for corporate stock, the latest publication relating to the Bureau's financial research.[1] In this report, a revised version of which will soon be published by the National Bureau, balance sheets for foundations and for colleges and universities are estimated and removed from the residual or household sector, and asset holdings of households are disaggregated by the age and wealth of the holder. As is frequently the case, the reexamination of existing data produced revisions that appeared to contradict some widely held beliefs, such as the assumption that the household sector's share in stock had been declining sharply throughout the years since World War II; it also suggested some questions for further study, such as those arising from the apparent finding that households' performance in the stock market was, in terms of capital gains, at least as good as, and probably better than, that of institutions.

[1] *Institutional Investors and Corporate Stock: A Background Study,* Institutional Investor Study Report of the Securities and Exchange Commission, Supplementary Volume I, Washington, D.C., U.S. Government Printing Office, March 10, 1971.

The second item of progress on the suggestions made at the meeting is the start, in 1971, of a major project on the effect of inflation on financial markets under a grant from the Life Insurance Association of America, the source of financing for so much of the research reviewed by Lintner. The project includes several studies. Lintner and John Piper, partly through interviews with portfolio managers to obtain information not publicly available, will examine changes in the investment policies and portfolios of several important types of financial institutions in response to inflation. Among the objects will be to ascertain the importance of new techniques, such as equity kickers, adopted by financial institutions to protect their assets against inflation.

Another study in this group, by Thomas Sargent, will attempt to measure the relations between price level changes and prices and yields on bonds and common stocks, using the experience of several different countries and periods. A third, by Stanley Diller, will study bonds convertible into common stock, considering them as one of the devices used for hedging against inflation. A comparison between yields on convertible bonds and yields on nonconvertible bonds with similar characteristics can be interpreted as a measure of expected changes in equity prices. Lester Taylor, in another of these studies, will look into the way in which households alter the distribution of their investments in response to inflation and expectations of inflation. In addition to these studies, some attention will also be directed to building up a historical record of stock price movements during inflationary periods in as wide a variety of countries and situations as possible.

The National Bureau, thanks to the participants in the colloquium, now has a large number of thoughtful recommendations for future research in finance and capital markets. We are grateful to John Lintner, to the chairman, Robert V. Roosa, the formal discussants, William J. Baumol, Sidney Homer, and James J. O'Leary, and to the Hon. Richard B. Smith, who addressed the dinner meeting, as well as all the participants in the informal discussion for their suggestions and guidance.

ROBERT E. LIPSEY
Vice President-Research

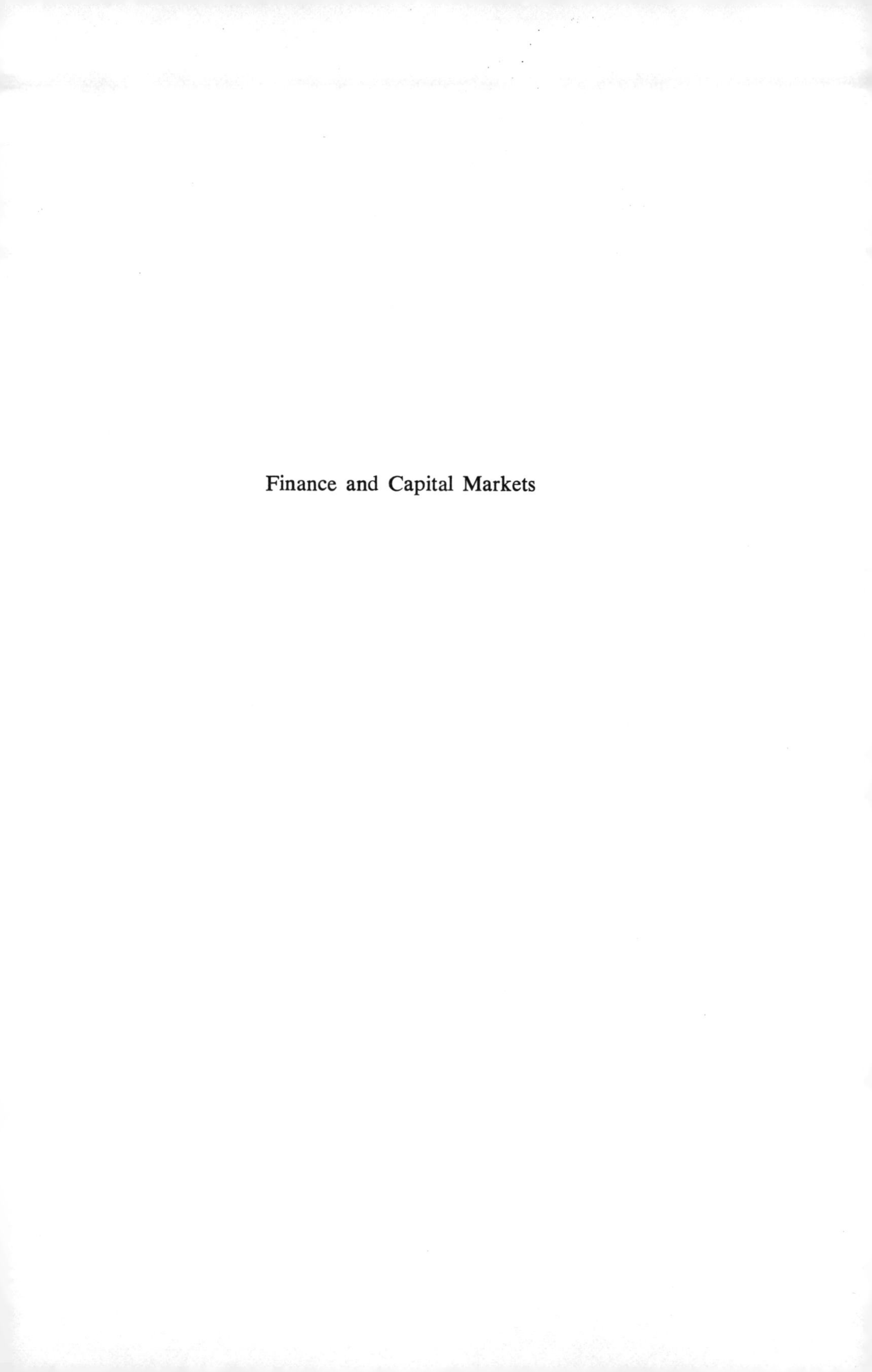

Finance and Capital Markets

Finance and Capital Markets

John Lintner
Harvard University

INTRODUCTION

Research on the ways economic activity is financed and the operations of financial institutions and markets has long played a major role in the work of the National Bureau. On the occasion of its Fiftieth Anniversary, this paper will survey the Bureau's work in these fields, and place it in the context of the state of knowledge at the time and some of the more important research being conducted elsewhere. The emphasis throughout this survey will be on the dominant trends, directions and contributions of the earlier research, and on certain significant gaps and shortcomings. In the final sections we undertake to identify major current problems and gaps in the core of our present knowledge and understanding that, in the context of our historical review, suggest certain major directions and basic strategies for future research.

The National Bureau's early pioneering work on the national income and its distribution and on the anatomy and physiology of business cycles was first supplemented by an organized *Program of Financial Research* in 1937. The Depression had emphasized the fundamental importance of a better understanding of financial organization and behavior and their relations to economic activity and issues of social welfare. A distinguished Exploratory Committee [1] was convened to examine how the Bureau could best organize and focus its research effort on these matters. After conducting an inventory of available data and research, the committee found an almost complete "lack of any conception of the most elementary magnitudes involved in the financial structure" [2] other

[1] The membership of the committee was Winfield W. Riefler, Chairman; David Friday, Walter Lichtenstein, and J. H. Riddle. The committee engaged Ralph A. Young to develop its inventory of relevant research and to act as its secretary, and Joseph H. Willits, Executive Director of the National Bureau also worked actively with the committee.

[2] This quotation is the summary of the 1937 committee's conclusions made by the 1964 exploratory committee [43, p. 1].

than traditional banking statistics, and particularly emphasized the lack of information on the "size, movement or structure" of the markets for consumer loans, urban mortgages, trade credits, and other sources of business financing (apart from short-term bank loans). It specifically recommended "projects in (such) areas where factual information and disinterested information are urgently needed at present," but more fundamentally, it emphasized that

> the time calls for *a new approach to the entire problem of finance,* an approach that is not limited to single institutions or to piecemeal legislation. . . . The primary need is to determine facts and establish principles. . . . A *comprehensive survey of the financial structure as a whole* is urgently needed to provide a background for the analysis of financial problems and to give perspective to proposals for changes in the financial structure. . . . This survey . . . must be sufficiently comprehensive, furthermore, to show not only *the structure and functions of these various* (listed) *types of financial organizations taken individually,* but also *their relative importance and their interdependence.* Without this basic financial survey . . . it is impossible to come to any well considered opinion concerning many of the most pressing financial problems of today.[3]

To a quite remarkable degree the *Report and Recommendations* of this first Exploratory Committee, made a third of a century ago, have set the tone and strategy for most of the Bureau's subsequent financial research activity. Its recommendations led immediately to the studies of consumer instalment credit, business financing, urban mortgage credit, and agricultural financing that comprised the initial *Program of Financial Research* reviewed below. A decade later, another committee recommended that these studies of the users and suppliers of major types of credit be rounded out in historical and cross-sectional perspective by what became the Bureau's postwar series on capital formation and financing (see section II). It also emphasized the need to determine "the origin, volume and composition of money savings in the United States . . . with greater precision and for a longer period of time than has so far been possible" [45, p. 4], in order to understand the flow of funds to institutions and the demand for securities. The 1937 committee's emphasis on the need to examine the relative importance and interde-

[3] The quotations are from pages 5 and 23 of [42]. Emphasis supplied.

pendence of financial instruments and institutions in the context of the financial structure as a whole, which was also reinforced by the 1946 committee, clearly called for the research which eventuated in the Bureau's later development of the flow-of-funds accounts, national balance sheets, and estimates of the magnitude and structure of the national wealth, which are reviewed in section III. In the context of this accumulating stock of organized knowledge, and following recommendations of review committees in 1954 [44] and 1964 [43], the Bureau then undertook a series of more intensive studies of the functioning of particular capital markets, which we review in section IV along with other related studies.

All this work represented a natural evolution of the original "vision" (in Schumpeter's phrase) of the founders of financial research at the Bureau a generation ago. My own recommendations in the final section can properly be regarded as carrying on the same line of development—albeit with certain major shifts in emphasis, focus, and methodology that are appropriate under new circumstances.

I. THE INITIAL FINANCIAL RESEARCH PROGRAM

Consumer Instalment Financing

Within three years of the initial proposals, Ralph Young and his associates had produced seven studies of this important but little known type of credit. The first five volumes were institutional studies of the major suppliers, namely *Personal Finance Companies* [157], *Sales Finance Companies* [126], *Commercial Banks* [16], *Government Agencies* [25] and *Industrial Banking Companies* [137]. In addition to developing data on its operations, each separate study described how the institution functions, its sources of financing, the different segments of the consumer market it serves, its credit practices and standards, as well as its legal regulation and the competitive influences on its operations. Duncan Holthausen [76] developed data at the Bureau on instalment credit granted, repayments, and outstandings for automobile dealers, department and furniture stores, appliance dealers, personal finance companies, industrial banking companies, and personal loan departments of commercial banks, by months beginning in 1929. He then joined the Department of Commerce where these important series were continued; to be later taken over by the Federal Reserve System. For the first time for any major financial market with the partial exception of S.E.C. data on the bond market, the Bureau had provided critically important time series data on both *gross* and *net flows* as well as *stocks outstanding*, all *disaggregated* by major industries.

But this valuable information on the structure and flows by, and through, supplier groups needed to be supplemented by corresponding information on the demand side of these markets. To meet this need, Bernstein [6] made a detailed cross-sectional analysis of the use of charge accounts, cash loans, and instalment credit (separately and in total) by the families covered in the large nationwide 1935–36 WPA-BLS Consumer Purchases Study. Although the quality of the raw sample data was recognized to be less than ideal, and provided a snapshot for only one year, critically important knowledge on the *structure of demand* for consumer credit by income groups, occupation, city size, and other economic and social characteristics was available for the first time. Indeed, recalling the lack of information regarding these markets noted by the Exploratory Committee just three years previously, the seven volumes of integrated but disaggregated and substantive research published in 1940 represented a quantum advance on anyone's scale in our knowledge of these important markets.

Three additional studies published in 1940–44 capped off this comprehensive investigation of consumer credit markets a generation ago. David Durand pioneered in the application of Hotelling's Discriminant Analysis to analyze the *Risk Elements in Consumer Instalment Financing* [40], using carefully designed samples of "good" and "bad" loans drawn from the files of several different groups of private lenders. Gottfried Haberler [67] prepared a classic study of how the introduction and use of this type of credit affects fluctuations in business activity at different stages of expansion or contraction, and their effects upon the banking system. Finally, Ernst Dauer [30] examined the *Comparative Operating Experience of Consumer Instalment Financing Agencies and Commercial Banks, 1929–41*.

Business Financing

A correspondingly integrated set of studies of credits to finance business operations was brought out in the years 1942–45. The first of four studies by Jacoby and Saulnier examined the rapid development of *Term Lending in Business* [81] on an amortizing basis by banks, insurance companies, and other lenders as an alternative to either short-term credits or long-term public bond issues; the others developed data and studied the evolving markets for *Accounts Receivable Financing* [133], *Financing Equipment for Commercial and Industrial Enterprises* [136], and *Financing Inventory on Field Warehouse Receipts* [80]. Merwin studied the *Financing and Economic Characteristics of Small Corporations in Five Manufacturing Industries, 1926–36* [110], devoting one section to the possible predictive and diagnostic value of deteriorations in certain credit ratios as predictors of impending insolvency.

In those days before the Compustat tapes, the Bureau laboriously tabulated balance sheet, income statement and source and application of funds data annually for 1920–39 for a sample of eighty-four larger manufacturing companies in eleven industries, fourteen large department stores, and thirteen other large trade corporations. Koch [90] used these data along with comparable information on railroads, telephones, and electric utilities, to make a comprehensive study of the changing chronological and cross-sectional patterns of the *Financing of Large Corporations, 1920–39.* Gross and net demands for funds were systematically related to the profitability of operations and to the scale of the investments being made in fixed assets, inventory, trade credit, and liquid funds (cash and marketable securities). Changes in the volumes and relative reliance on funds from operations, trade credit, bank borrowing and security issues were traced and related to differences in the asset and liability structure of balance sheets among industries and overtime. Among the surprising findings was the fact that even though "security sales fluctuate with general business activity and . . . have decreased over the period, . . . during years of equivalent business activity, however, security sales during the thirties were as large, if not larger, than in the twenties." [90, p. 6] (cf. Berle and Means!) Also, large manufacturers had been net purchasers rather than net sellers of securities during the twenties but were net sellers (issuers) rather than net buyers in the thirties. If this surprised (and called for explanation by) students of finance, the factual analysis also turned up something for the macro-Keynesians by showing that over the period as a whole, "our sample of industrial giants financed the major part of their operations without drawing on the savings of the public." Altogether, this was a pioneering, benchmark study richly pregnant with facts and suggested structural relations calling for later more sophisticated theoretical and econometric investigation, such as that undertaken within a few years by Meyer and Kuh [111], and the rapidly growing body of work which has followed.

The Koch study was soon complemented by Lutz' study [103] of the behavior of *Corporate Cash Balances, 1914–43,* using the same data for large corporations, supplemented by a sample of medium and small manufacturing and trade companies in Wisconsin. Lutz related changes in cash balances (and marketable securities) to changes in other major balance sheet items, during two wars and peacetime expansions and contractions, using the source and application of funds technique. This study was broadly related to the cash balances approach of classical monetary theory and more directly to the newer L_1 and L_2 Keynesian liquidity preference analysis applied to the corporate sector. Specifically, Lutz estimated transactions balances by applying the average ratio of the 1920's to payments in each year. He then examined the behavior of residual balances in relation to reliance on bank credit, and emphasized many important differences in the movements of residual cash balances and marketable securities at various times. He also found major differences in the patterns for large corporations relative to those of smaller companies, as well as significant contrasts between the payments velocity of corporations and that of the total economy. Although we now know from the work of Baumol [4] and Tobin [149] roughly a decade later that the transactions demand for cash balances is also a function of interest rates and not simply proportional to outlays—as Keynes had specified and Lutz had assumed in preparing his estimates—the work does represent one of the notable early attempts at the Bureau to use a formal economic model in the preparation and analysis of financial data.

These important studies were also complemented by Chudson's detailed cross-sectional study [17] of the asset and financial structure of some threescore industrial subgroupings of companies in manufacturing, mining, trade, and construction. Detailed unpublished tabulations of tax returns for the 1937 statistics of income were used to make comparisons of numerous ratios of asset and liability items by industry and size groups, and separately for income and deficit companies. Since comparative balance sheet and income statements were not available for the companies in any group, the study had to be confined to ratios and could not proceed to a comparison of sources and application of funds by industrial groups, as Koch had done. Nevertheless, the study documented the absence of normal or typical ratios for the economy as a whole, but found significant clusterings within particular industry, size, and profitability groups. It concluded that "As criteria for credit analysis (or, we may add, as inputs into more modern econometric studies of risk), financial ratios take on significance only when compared within a given class of concerns or when examined for the same group of firms over a period of time" [17, p. 6].

Jacoby and Saulnier in *Business Financing and Banking* [79], described as "the capstone study of the Business Financing project" (p. vii), then integrated the results of these (and other [4]) studies of the broad changes that had taken place in the financial needs of business during the long period from 1900–45 and how various financial institutions, commercial banks in particular, adapted to these changing demands. The development and activities of government lending and insuring agencies in the latter part of the period were also examined. Short-term working capital loans had made up more than half the earning assets of commercial banks before World War I, but had undergone a large and progressive decline over the following quarter century. Such developments were carefully related to shifts in the industry mix and sectoral structure of the economy and changes in the size distribution of business firms, as well as to the development of newer longer-term forms of credit better adapted to the changing needs of business firms. Very significantly, the authors on the basis of their analysis concluded in 1947 that commercial banks would fully maintain and probably enlarge their position as suppliers of business credit in the postwar world. Although this was a minority view at the time, it was based on perceptive research and has of course been borne out to a remarkable degree in the developments in the postwar period.

Another major general conclusion of this work has also been well sustained by more recent history. After noting that funds retained from operations generally satisfy business demands for funds when assets are expanding at a low or moderate rate, the authors conclude that the demand for external funds will be substantial whenever the expansion of assets is "at a high, *and particularly at an accelerating rate.*" [79, p. 7, underscoring added.] In keeping with the National Bureau's style and technology at the time this perceptive generalization was left in verbal form, however, it clearly implies important nonlinearities [5] for formal models of business demands for funds in the money and capital markets which have not even yet been fully exploited in later statistical investigations.

Four years after this "capstone study" an econometric examination of *Corporate Income Retention, 1915–43* was prepared by Dobrovolsky

[4] Notably, [84] and [1].

[5] We may add that it also implies potentially significant discontinuities in the first (or second) derivatives of the demand functions, or conditioning on "state of the world" variables that have not been carefully formulated and tested in later work.

[35], using statistics of income data for manufacturing companies and samples of large and small corporations. Dobrovolsky found that corporations had positive net savings (or dissavings) when profits were above (or below) a 5 per cent return on book net worth, and that they had had a stable (linear) marginal propensity to save between 70 and 80 cents of each dollar of profits per hundred dollars of net worth. In addition to profits on net worth, he found that previous rates of dividends on book value and to a lesser degree current rates of asset expansion relative to net worth were secondary though significant shift variables [6] in the corporate savings function. Dobrovolsky clearly formulated a model of the decision-making behavior he was studying, and proceeded to test its validity and estimate the parameters of the model he used. Given the state of knowledge and statistical practice at that time, the scientific quality of the work was high. This judgment need not be altered by the fact that within a few years Lintner [98], on the basis of detailed interviews with a carefully structured sample of companies, developed a radically different model of dividend behavior that proved to be statistically very much more satisfactory.[7]

Urban Mortgage Credit

The third major area of financial activity emphasized by the Exploratory Committee in 1937 as requiring massive empirical-institutional investigation was the field of urban mortgages—"probably the largest single category of credit in our financial system" [42, p. 19]. By 1941, David Wickens [155] had been able to compile a valuable source book of data on *Residential Real Estate: Its Economic Position as Shown by Values, Rents, Family Incomes, Financing and Construction.* The book's 250 pages of tables were based largely on information from recent government surveys as well as additional work by the Bureau, and were supported by 50 pages of text that noted gaps and limitations of available data. The study also showed that land and buildings accounted for more than half the national wealth, that residential property dominated all real estate, and that residential mortgages were much the largest single form of credit outstanding. Wickens also emphasized the wide regional differences and fluctuations in real estate markets that make generalizations for the country as a whole dangerous.

[6] He also found that the earned surplus position, introduced earlier by Tinbergen [147], had some effect on retentions, but this was marginal and less conclusive.

[7] For later work on this subject, see [11], [97], [46], and [153].

A decade later, Ernest Fisher [50] in a comprehensive survey of *Urban Real Estate Markets* was able to fill in many of the informational gaps Wickens had noted earlier. Although the real estate market is really "a series of localized, fragmentized, and particularized markets for a wide variety of rights to assorted services flowing from numerous unique sources, and only roughly comparable one with the other" (p. 12), Fisher identifies major groupings and examines their economic characteristics and different patterns of financing, along with the influence of changing financing terms (loan-value ratios, interest rates, etc.) and incomes on behavior in each market. The quality of the analysis of these matters may be illustrated by one perceptive conclusion that has been notably confirmed over the past two decades. In discussing the effect of liberalized credit terms on the prices of residential real estate, Fisher finds

> In a buyer's market . . . when there is an opportunity to select from a number of homes having about the same price and quality, more liberal credit probably raises housing standards; but in a seller's market, when choice is restricted . . . more liberal credit is likely to be absorbed in price with probably a reduction in housing standards [50, p. 88].

Along with such institutionally informed and sound applied economic analysis, Fisher helped establish a richer and more systematic framework that would aid and stimulate further investigations of real estate markets.

About the same time as Fisher's work, Miles Colean provided further perspective in a systematic survey of *The Impact of Government on Real Estate Finance in the United States* [19] from the early agrarian period (with land policies strongly emphasizing individual ownership of small tracts and state intervention to limit distress to mortgage borrowers), through the beginnings of federal intervention and action with the Federal Land Bank system in 1916, to the pervasive federal activities of the 1930's—which included the creation of the Federal Home Loan Bank system in 1932, the federal chartering and insuring of accounts in federal savings and loan associations, and the operations of the Federal Housing Administration, which limited lender's risks by insuring that mortgage loans meet certain new standards of credit appraisal that were rapidly adopted by lending institutions in making their uninsured residential loans as well. The study also traced and examined the increasing use of mortgage credit to encourage home ownership to influence the volume of residential construction and to control the quality of land planning, housing design, and construction. The federal government's response to the emergency created by the massive foreclosures of the 1930's was ably examined in Lowell Harris' *History and Policies of the Home Owners' Loan Corporation* [68].

The Bureau's research on urban mortgage financing also included major studies of the supply side of the market. Saulnier [138] examined the shifting role of life insurance companies in different parts of the residential and commercial mortgage markets, both as percentages of company assets and of total market supply of each type, and analyzed the gross and net yields, operating costs, foreclosure, and loss experience of these lenders on different types of loans made at different times. Behrens [5] made a similar study of *Commercial Bank Activities* in these markets. Earlier, Lintner [100] had independently made a similar detailed study of the operations and experience of *Mutual Savings Banks in the Savings and Mortgage Markets.* A few years later, Morton [118] drew on all this earlier work (and the unpublished work by Edwards on savings and loan associations) to present a comprehensive summary of the major changes and trends in urban mortgage markets over the period 1920–53, emphasizing comparisons by lending institution and type of property as well as loan characteristics (amortization, contract length, loan-value ratio, etc.). For each type of lending institution, both foreclosure rates and realized percentage losses were significantly higher on income properties than on 1–4 family residential loans, and within each type of property they rose regularly and rapidly with the initial loan-value ratio, with size of loan, and with size of community. Mortgages made to middle-aged borrowers had much more favorable experience than those made to either young or older debtors.

On the basis of his survey of loans currently outstanding (about 1950), Morton finds that the roughly 40 per cent of all this debt covered by federal insurance or guarantee was concentrated on homes and properties and borrowers in an intermediate economic position judging by the borrower's incomes, value of property, and occupation of the owner; while conventional loans predominated at the upper and lower ends of the scales. As Saulnier observes in his introduction, "the best experience during the trying years of the thirties was on the very types of loans that are now most frequently protected by federal loan insurance or guarantees . . . and that the least favorable experience was on those that are still made predominantly without such protection" [138, p. 6].

These studies of mortgage lending experience also provided very tangible evidence suggesting systematic and pervasive deteriorations in the quality of credits extended during long sustained periods of prosperity. Specifically, the fractions of mortgages made in each year that were subsequently in default—and the fractions that were subsequently foreclosed and, in particular, the losses taken as a percentage of lender's investments in the loans—all increased throughout the 1920's and were highest on the loans made in 1927–29. This was true for each type of lending institution. For loans requiring regular reductions of principal, these patterns could be interpreted as merely confirming the well known proposition that seasoned loans that have been substantially amortized are of better quality than unseasoned and unamortized loans. But the more significant and sharper result was that the same patterns were found in the experience of each type of lender with loans on each kind of property, when only those loans which provided for *no* amortization of principal were considered.

These studies also provided significant evidence regarding the extent to which differences in interest rates charged different classes of mortgagors properly compensate for the differences in losses subsequently realized. Out of twenty-seven comparisons of differences in interest rates and in loss rates (fifteen for insurance companies and twelve for commercial banks),

> there were 12 cases in which the differences in contract rates were the *opposite* of what subsequent experience shows would have been necessary to correct for differences in losses. In 15 cases the differences in contract rates were in the right direction, but 13 of these were less than what subsequent experience showed to be necessary. In short, the lenders made the wrong adjustments about as frequently as they made the right ones, and where they made the right ones, they almost always failed to go as far as they should. Life insurance experience in this respect was almost exactly the same as that of commercial banks (p. 12).

Lintner [100, tables 41–43] had earlier shown the same disparate patterns in mutual savings banks experience.

Since reasonable allowance for differences in costs would be substantially smaller than the differences in realized losses, the explanation for these findings must rather be found in other directions. In particular, experience with different classes of mortgages made by the same set of lenders under quite similar competitive conditions leaves little doubt that *ex ante* expectations were seriously and differentially *biased estimates* of *ex post* results—contrary to the famous "rational expectations hypothesis" later advanced by Muth [122] and used as a *premise* in much subsequent econometric work.[8] At the same time, other features of the record clearly point up the importance of differences in the competitive structure or the industrial organization of the supply side of major parts of the over-all mortgage market, and of corresponding differences in the information and sophistication among potential borrowers.[9]

Finally, in addition to all these comprehensive and pioneering studies of consumer instalment credit, business financing and urban mortgages, the Bureau's initial program of financial research as conceived in the *Report* of the Exploratory Committee in 1937 was rounded out by a shorter group of studies on agricultural financing. Saulnier [134] examined *Costs and Returns on Farm Mortgage Lending by Life Insurance Companies,* and Diesslin studied *Agricultural Equipment Financing* [33]. Jones and Durand [82] in *Mortgage Lending Experience in Agriculture* combined significant original research with a careful analysis of studies done elsewhere, and Horton [77] broke important new ground in his cross-sectional analysis of the economic and physical determinants of the *Patterns of Farm Financial Structure.*

In an overview, the studies in the Bureau's program of financial research accomplished their objectives to an exemplary degree. They systematically built up a very substantial and well organized body of knowledge regarding the users and suppliers of major types of credit in the economy about which little was previously known with any detail or precision. They examined the characteristics and impact of important new techniques of financing user assets, and they placed these in the

[8] As illustrations, single family and 3–4 family homes in Massachusetts carried the same average interest rate (5.94 per cent), but the net loss to the total amount loaned was nearly twice as large on the latter (8.6 per cent vs. 4.6 per cent). Similarly, the average interest charged on combination apartments and stores (5.89 per cent) was less than on "pure" apartments (5.99 per cent), and lending costs were approximately the same, but 2.42 per cent per annum would have been required to provide for subsequent losses on the former as against 1.37 per cent per annum on simple apartments [Lintner 100, tables 41, 43].

[9] Average contract interest on 1–4 family residence loans in Massachusetts was 5.95 per cent with annual *ex post* reserve requirements of 0.48 per cent; average interest on income property loans was 5.80 per cent and *ex post* loss reserve requirements were 1.54 per cent per annum. Differences in other lending costs were at most .2–.3 percent [Lintner 100, p. 362].

context of the continuing usage of more established forms of finance in each market. They developed revealing cross-sectional profiles of the reliance on different types of financing in terms of borrower characteristics, and the market shares of different types of lending institutions in different major credit markets. They included important analytical results on the risk characteristics of consumer credits, and major studies of lender losses and realized returns on mortgage loans on residences, apartment houses and other income producing properties. In the Koch, Lutz, Jacoby-Saulnier, and Dobrovolsky studies of business financing, effective use was made of the newly emerging accounting frameworks of sources and application of funds to develop valuable raw data from balance sheets and income statements, and to organize the information. Important features were uncovered of the behavior of bank debt, retained funds and reliance on outside longer-terms debt and equity financing over time by different size and industry groupings of firms. Moreover, at least first order explanations in the true scientific sense of both the observed cross-sectional differences in financing patterns between groups and the time series variations within groups were developed and presented.

Without reopening the famous "facts without theory" controversy regarding the Bureau's work on business cycles,[10] which falls outside the scope of our review, we may appropriately observe that any similar charge with respect to the Bureau's early and contemporaneous program of financial research would clearly overstate the situation, if it did not entirely miss the mark. To be sure, the theory used was in most cases qualitative and rather general, but this intellectual framework of relations between demands and supplies, assets and liabilities, balance sheets, income statements, and fund flows *sufficed to organize the search for the data* and other empirical facts that were essential inputs for later stages of scientific analysis. It is surely no disparagement to say that the greatest contribution of this series of early studies was its impressive body of organized information about financial markets. After all, Darwin, and other zoologists, had to observe and study the animals before he could come up with the theory of evolution! Moreover, specific theoretical models were used in preparing estimates and interpreting the data, as noted in the work of Lutz and Dobrovolsky. While the prior theoretical input to the statistical estimates of behavioral relations in the other studies often took the form of statements of various fundamental

[10] See [91], [13], [155] and [131].

canons of finance, these canons had their analytical rationales, which generally make good sense to modern theorists. A good and revealing illustration is provided by the use in several of these studies of the proposition that it is generally desirable to match the maturities of liabilities or other sources of funds to the "duration" [11] of the assets being held or financed. Without being graced by the title of Habitat Theory, conferred much more recently by Modigliani and Sutch [114] in their study of the term structure of interest rates—and (again as in the Modigliani-Sutch usage) without explicitly deriving the proposition from a modern mathematical formulation positing von Neumann-Morganstern utility maximization subject to constraints—it was nevertheless *genuine theory that put hypothesized structure on the data.* Over two decades later, we should expect sophisticated work to formulate dynamic multivariate stock-flow adjustment models of these phenomena and to estimate reaction parameters by the methods that are appropriate to stochastic systems of equations. But these theoretical and statistical models were unknown at the time, and our knowledge of them must not blind us to the scientific character of this earlier work.

II. STUDIES IN CAPITAL FORMATION AND FINANCING

This major new series undertaken in 1950 under Kuznets' direction [12] gave valuable longer term perspective to the ongoing studies in the Bureau's initial Program of Financial Research. Grebler, Blank, and Winnick [62] examined the strategic, demographic, and economic factors determining the secular trends and long-term cycles in residential construction over the period 1889–1953. On the basis of much new data they highlighted the declining long-term trend in the ratio of this form of capital formation in real terms to the total output and real capital formation in the economy, and they also observed persistent declines in the amount of real capital invested per dwelling unit. They also showed that there had been adverse changes in relative prices, and strong trends toward greater use of debt for the purchase of new dwellings as well as the acquisition and reconditioning of existing structures. As a result, residential mortgage debt had shown a marked secular increase per capita and per household and as a fraction of total private long-term

[11] As noted below Macaulay [105] in his study of interest rates had earlier developed the refined and precise concept of duration.

[12] This series was financed by a large grant from the Life Insurance Association of America through the good offices of Dr. James J. O'Leary.

debt, personal income, and the value of all residential real estate. Alvin Tostlebe [152] prepared a companion study of *The Formation and Financing of Capital in Agriculture Since 1870,* and Melville Ulmer [154] examined the corresponding trends and long cycles in investment and methods of financing used in transportation, communications, and public utilities.

Ulmer found marked retardation rates of growth of real capital and substantial declines in both average and marginal capital-output coefficients [13] in all industries (the declines in telephones being smallest). He also found a "pronounced and progressive shift over time" toward reliance on internal financing (again the shift was least in telephones), as well as a strong and pervasive shift in the *form* of external financing from stocks to bonds. The growing reliance on internal funds was analytically explained by the (diminishing) inadequacies of depreciation changes over several decades and the decline in rates of real capital growth.

Creamer, Dobrovolsky, and Borenstein [28] made a similar study of the manufacturing and mining industries. Both output and capital showed higher rates of growth than the economy as a whole, but the growth of both output and capital in these industries showed marked retardation. The capital-output ratios in most industrial branches in manufacturing and mining had risen until 1919, and then had persistently fallen almost synchronously in different industries over time. With respect to financing, they showed that internal funds had been rising relative to plant and equipment outlays, but that they had nevertheless been secularly stable as a percentage of all sources of funds during the first half of this century.[14]

Kuznets in his introduction developed a model to explain these observed trends in (gross) capital-output ratios in terms of technological change and rates of growth of output. The model implies differences in

[13] These declines were interpreted in terms of indivisibility of capital units, strongly increasing returns to scale, the need to build facilities to anticipate demand, and capital-saving technological change. As Borts [10] notes in his contemporary review, Ulmer's effort to find any effect of changes in relative prices of labor and capital fails because his reliance on real rates and an index of long-term interest rates does not allow for the effects of initial purchase price and expected life on the costs of capital goods. We may add that the relevant "cost of capital" depends also on the cost of equity money. It is understated by market interest rates on bonds and, more significantly in this context, has often shown substantially different changes over substantial periods of time.

[14] See also Lintner [99], Sametz [132], Kuznets [92], and Shapiro [140].

the time paths of fixed capital output ratios and working capital-output ratios which are confirmed by the data. Moreover, since the need for financing varies directly with the marginal capital-output ratio, while the average ratio (given the depreciation rate) determines the contribution of depreciation to internal funds, the model also explains the observed patterns in the mix of financing, assuming profit rate and dividend payout ratios are constant on average.

The capstone volume in this important series was Kuznets' *Capital in the American Economy: Its Formation and Financing* [92], which integrated the findings of these earlier studies with additional data he developed to provide country-wide totals. Capital stocks and capital-output ratios were estimated in current and constant dollars, both gross and net of depreciation, and in relation to output, population, and labor force. The structure of capital formation was analyzed by type of capital good and category of uses (business, households, and governments) and by industrial sector, while gross and net internal funds, outside equity, and short- and long-term debt were distinguished for each sector. As in the earlier monographs, the focus was on developing objective empirical findings based on detailed evidence regarding the secular trends and the Kuznets-Burns long cycles of each of these magnitudes, and the apparent relations between different constructs and classifications.

This study is universally recognized as an indispensable and classic reference for all concerned with the shifting structures of capital formation and financing, which have been associated with the past growth of the economy, and the light these cast upon its future prospects. Although the author himself modestly describes the study in his introduction (page 7) as "largely a compound of estimation and classification seasoned at different levels of empirical findings with conjectural explanation, and topped off with a frosting of impressionistic speculation," the interpretive analysis, theoretical modeling [15] and indeed the informed speculations of so wise a scholar are a rich store of refutable hypotheses for subsequent research, even when the insights offered fail to be complete or final truths.

The inherently complex issues raised by any attempt to identify and measure the determinants of magnitude and allocation of an economy's savings through its institutional channels—and their interaction with demographic, technological, and other economic determinants of the structure of demands for capital—require something more than the

[15] As an illustration, recall the model relating the average and marginal capital-output ratios to trends in the mix of financing mentioned in the previous paragraph.

framework provided by the national income accounts for their analysis. Moreover, we all recognize that the fundamental perspective provided by knowledge and understanding of long-run cycles and trends is not sufficient to meet many of our important policy needs. We now turn to the Bureau's important work developing flow-of-funds accounts and sectorized national balance sheets as complements to the framework of national income accounts it developed earlier, through the efforts of Kuznets and his associates.

III. FLOWS OF FUNDS AND NATIONAL BALANCE SHEETS

The studies in the Bureau's initial *Program of Financial Research* had been directed to the mandate of the 1937 Exploratory Committee [16] to displace ignorance with firm empirical knowledge of the size, movement, and structure of major credit markets and, together with the Kuznets capital formation series, had provided a great deal of the perspective which had been called for. But perspective is a cross-sectional as well as a time-series concept, and it will be recalled that this early Exploratory Committee had also heavily emphasized the fundamental importance of *"a comprehensive survey of the financial structure as a whole* [(including detailed studies of) the activities . . . structure and functions (of a long list) of financial organizations and markets taken individually] and also their relative importance *and their interdependence."* The studies of Copeland and Goldsmith reviewed in this section, together with the subsequent and ongoing work of Brill and his associates in the Federal Reserve's division of research, have made monumental contributions to developing the conceptual frameworks and detailed data required by this coordinate mandate of the 1937 Committee. In the following section we will review the Bureau's studies of individual institutions and markets called for in the portion of the quotation we have bracketed above.

Copeland's Moneyflows

In view of the knowledge of the flow-of-funds accounts that most readers of this paper will have, and the substantial development and refinement they have undergone since Copeland's pioneering work on *Moneyflows* [24] in 1952, it is appropriate to focus on the genesis and character of the achievement. As Riefler notes in his introduction,

[16] See above.

> This . . . extraordinary inquiry . . . is the product of a lifetime of probing into the meaning and significance of money, and of delving into and improving statistical material essential to analysis of how money does in fact flow through our economy. . . . [It] echoes his earlier absorption with accounting . . . [and his] preoccupation with theoretical formulations and his insistence that they be subject to empirical verification [24, p. ix].

Copeland had become intensely interested in accounting along with economics as a graduate student and before taking his degree published a study of "Seasonal Problems in Financial Administration" of individual firms based on an analysis of cash budgets [23]. In Washington [17] during the early 1920's, he had sought to identify the transactions that properly belonged in Fisher's celebrated equation of exchange MV=PT. He argued that the appropriate money circuit encompassed more than final purchases of goods and services (because many identifiable financial transactions affected the latter), but excluded many other transactions.[18] While seeking to analyze his data to determine probable causal relationships, he incorporated the primitive national income data the Bureau was just beginning to provide and put his money circuit measurements in social accounting terms. Along the way he produced an early consolidated balance sheet for the banking sector [21] and unpublished memoranda which "fit cash balances into an imaginary set of sector accounts." About a decade later (1942–43) he began to put "actual figures for sector accounts together on an aggregative basis somewhat long the lines . . ." later published.[19]

The National Bureau in 1944 invited Copeland to undertake an exploratory project to determine what could be done to provide a fuller statistical picture of the money circuit. The project was undertaken at the request of the C.E.D., which provided generous financing for two years. Copeland's introduction credits Theodore O. Yntema with originally conceiving and arranging for the project, as well as providing "the

[17] Copeland spent several years in the Division of Research and Statistics of the Federal Reserve Board, headed by Riefler. See Riefler's introduction [24, p. ix].

[18] See [23, pp. 9–10]. Riefler's introduction [24, p. ix] also refers to the bearing on Copeland's later work of "his days as Executive Secretary of the Central Statistical Board where he operated so effectively to improve the quality, the comparability and the coverage of American economic statistics, and thus make it possible for others, as well as himself, to undertake a study as elaborate as this."

[19] The phrases quoted in the last two sentences are from the author's preface, p. xiii.

most useful criticism (anyone offered) of an early draft form of the financial statement here adopted." Wesley Mitchell prepared an unpublished memorandum for the guidance of the study, and Copeland states that "we have developed money-flow estimates in the form of a set of accounts for the United States that conforms on the whole quite closely to the specifications" given (in Mitchell's memorandum),[20] with eleven instead of only four sectors, but classifying moneyflows principally by object of expenditure.[21] Yntema, Mitchell, Riefler, Stewart, Young, and Brill all helped with advice and criticism at different stages of the planning and development of the study—and an able staff headed by Daniel H. Brill made the detailed number-work possible. To quote Riefler's introduction once more,

> . . . To those who have followed . . . this intricate study of moneyflows in the U.S. during the years 1936–42 . . . in its inception and progress, the great achievement is that Copeland has "pulled it off." He has shown that statistics do exist, on an annual basis at least, to support a construction of moneyflows for the entire economy of the U.S. by major sectors and by significant categories. The system he has developed incorporates not only current productive activity and the distribution and transfer of income, but also those transactions which help finance income transfer and production flows.
>
> The moneyflows system enables economists for the first time to view an integrated picture of the economy where the functioning of our monetary and credit system can be studied in conjunction with other economic developments. It demonstrates that with judicious and imaginative handling available statistics permit economists to go further than most of us had thought possible in constructing

[20] Excerpts from Mitchell's memorandum of June 1944 are quoted, with Copeland's comment in the text, in [24, p. 3].

[21] Mitchell's memorandum had proposed:

> For each group, we imagine that a double-entry account is kept. On one side, the account shows all payments received by units in the group. These payments are classified by (1) unit and group making the payment, (2) that for which the payment is received, and (3) form of currency in which the payment is received. On the other side, the account shows all payments made by units in the group, with expenditures classified in a corresponding fashion.

Only (2) was implemented in [24]. Mitchell had also proposed "A sharp line would be drawn between the payments made and received by an individual as a consumer and as a business man . . ."—a matter on which much more work is *still* needed.

a sweeping yet detailed picture of economic behavior. . . . The use of GNP "models" in explaining relationships between economic variables has become widespread. Copeland's work will expand the frontier of "model building" [24, pp. ix–x].

Although Copeland in this classic work did not push on to the construction and estimation of statistical models in the modern econometric sense, he did include a rich and suggestive discussion of the consistency requirements imposed by the combination of moneyflow and national income accounting. In particular, he related the accounting of moneyflows through financial channels to savings and investment account in national income statements, and carefully examined the relations of the banking sector to the moneyflows of all other transactors. He very constructively traced some of the widening ramifications through this complex accounting framework of decisions of "bulls" or "bears" to reduce cash balances, borrow or sell securities in order to increase or decrease their own outlays on goods, and the cumulative amplifying effects imposed on fluctuations by currently allowing for the behavior of "sheep" (followers whose outlays are ordinarily closely related to their incomes). He also undertook to use his detailed scheme of moneyflows accounts, and these analyses of their interactions and operation, to reexamine and restructure earlier, primarily American,[22] monetary theory. Although his reformulation of monetary theory per se is of little interest today, it is quite relevant in appraising his work to emphasize his *concern* with the structure of explanatory hypotheses, which would best account for the observed movements of the numbers within his elaborated accounting frameworks.

Just as Kuznets' great work in developing the national income

[22] In view of the significance Copeland attached to some transactors being "bulls" or "bears," it is surprising that he did not incorporate Keynes' "bearishness function" from the *Treatise* into his analysis to enrich its behavioral-motivational content. (As Lintner has pointed out [101, pp. 515–18], the liquidity preference function of the *general theory* was much less satisfactory.) Part of the explanation for this omission is doubtless found in the heritage of Copeland's lifelong effort to refine and develop Fisher's approach by way of the equation of exchange and his preference for loanable funds theories of interest rates. But if Copeland had taken this alternative route, his "bulls" or "bears" could then have been directly defined as transactors whose *functions* had shifted to the left or right, and their new positions would have provided one of the conditions for the final set of market adjustments. Alternatively, appropriate shift parameters could have been introduced as added explanatory variables in a composite demand for money function—as was developed subsequently in the work of many more recent authors.

accounts can never be faulted by the fact that he did not also create Keynes' *General Theory*—Copeland's tremendous achievement in producing the moneyflows accounts should not be faulted on the grounds that he did not also bring forth the rich integrating theories of portfolio balance and of capital marketing equilibrium under uncertainty that were developed many years later. Though Copeland failed to provide a satisfactory theory concerning the generation of the disequilibria evidenced by "bulls" or "bears" at any given time, I shall argue below that our theoretical and empirical understanding of the formulation of expectations—and, in particular, the determinants of *shifts* in expectations—is still rather primitive and uncertain. Copeland's theoretical effort, however inadequate it may otherwise seem by modern standards, at least had the merit of constructively focusing on the interrelated sequential adjustments of financial and other markets. His work for the first time created and implemented the crucial counting frameworks within which these dynamic processes must work themselves out.

The Bureau's early work culminating in Copeland's *Moneyflows* has been continued and substantially developed by Brill and Taylor heading the flow of funds section of the Division of Research of the Federal Reserve in Washington. By 1955, annual estimates for 1939–53 were published; annual statements of financial assets and liabilities by major sectors were added in 1959, and the accounts of flows of funds, savings, and investment were placed on a quarterly basis, although at the cost of sacrificing important information on gross flows. In 1958, the Bureau through a special committee chaired by Raymond Goldsmith [123] reviewed the current status of flow-of-funds and other national accounts, identified directions of needed further development, and examined the problems involved in achieving a fuller integration with other national accounts. It also devoted an entire conference in its Income and Wealth series [124] to the *Flow-of-Funds Approach to Social Accounting* with major papers and important comments by most of the leading scholars concerned with this work. The Board subsequently developed seasonally adjusted estimates of the flow of funds [8] and has further revised the accounts within the last five years [9] and [7]. Taylor [145] has published a description of the use of these accounts within the Federal Reserve System as of 1963. Some of the more recent analytical work for internal information is doubtless reflected in their partial incorporation in the financial sector of the MIT-FRM econometric model [129], [32], [31] to which we revert below.

For all concerned with the study of money, finance, and capital markets with their effects upon real economic activity, the Bureau's pioneering development of flows-of-funds accounts must rank in importance with its earlier work by Mitchell and Kuznets on the conceptualization and estimation of the national income accounts themselves. But sound financial analysis and planning in business requires examination and projection of balance sheet data,[23] as well as the information in income statements and exhibits of sources and uses of funds. In studying the workings and structure of the economy as a whole, knowledge of such balancing statements of *stocks* of wealth by type and claims by type can be no less important.[24] Once again, the Bureau has pioneered in developing the national wealth and balance sheets required. Indeed, apart from annual estimates of financial assets and liabilities provided, with a lag, by the Federal Reserve in connection with its flow-of-funds data, the impressive studies of Goldsmith and his associates represent almost all the profession's stock of capital of this type.

Goldsmith's Savings, Wealth and Balance Sheets

As with Copeland's *Moneyflows,* Goldsmith's great contributions at the Bureau grew out of his earlier interests and work. After early studies of the German [53] and American [52] banking systems, he had gone to the S.E.C. where he had prepared, with the assistance of Walter Salant, the first careful and reasonably satisfactory estimates of the volume and composition of individuals' saving.[25] The annual estimates were built up from balance sheet and other data on asset ownership for 1933–37. The Bureau published these results in volume 3 of its Income and Wealth series [61] in 1939. Then, after the war, Goldsmith undertook and brought forth his classic *Study of Saving in the United States* [60] with the objective of providing a comprehensive quantitative description, as well as an analysis, of the saving process in the United States in the first half of this century, i.e., of *the process of financing* the coun-

[23] This will doubtless seem more obvious to many in the financial community following the "Rediscovery of the Balance Sheet" by analysts and advisers on Wall Street during the first half, especially in May and June, of this year.

[24] Dorrance [36] reminds us that J. R. Hicks in *The Social Framework* (1942)—the first undergraduate text based on national income accounting—found it necessary to include a chapter on the national balance sheet, estimated as best he could.

[25] The characterization is found (p. 3) in Friend's later study [51] which grew out of and substantially extended Goldsmith's early work at the S.E.C. (Emphasis was added in the quotation.)

try's economic growth.[26] The work was truly "a monumental study, in the tradition of Bowley and Kuznets," [27] complete with 850 pages of tables, all neatly indexed and cross-referred to insure reproducibility, and 1042 pages [28] of textual exegesis and analysis. His extensive and imaginative use of balance sheet and wealth data in a context of the inherent relationships of the social accounting framework, enabled him to build up alternative estimates of savings over the period back to 1929, which provided important checks on the reliability of the largely residual savings estimates in the usual national income accounts.[29] They enabled him to derive savings estimates over the first three decades of the century for which national income accounts were available only in very rough form, and, most important for students of finance, this approach provided essential detail concerning the *composition and disposition* of the savings being made in the economy. Moreover, by drawing on the extensive sets of balance sheet and wealth data being developed for the estimates of savings, Goldsmith was able to provide informed alternative estimates of savings that are potentially very useful because of their economic and motivational relevance, even though they depart from the usual social and national income accounting concepts. Important examples are the estimates inclusive of capital gains or losses, and estimates of net personal and business savings based on different estimates of depreciation (straight-line or other time patterns based on original or reproduction costs).

This great *Study of Savings* was soon followed by Goldsmith's well-known study of *Financial Intermediaries* [54], which integrated all the available asset and liability data for the individual institutions, spanning considerably more than half a century, into a consistent set of accounts focusing on their relationships with each other and their systematic relations to the saving and financing of the ultimate suppliers

[26] *Ibid.*, Preface, p. ix. Underscoring added. This work was also financed by the Life Insurance Association of America through Dr. James J. O'Leary, its Director of Research, who served as Secretary to the Advisory Committee for the Study, with Dr. Winfield W. Riefler as Chairman. Goldsmith in his preface speaks of this special appreciation for the contributions of both to his work.

[27] The quoted phrase introduces James Morgan's Review Article on Goldsmith's study in the *American Economic Review* [116].

[28] Not including 240 pages in volume III (Brady's study of "Family Saving 1888–1950," and Mendershausen's "Pattern of Estate Tax Wealth").

[29] Copeland [23, p. 340] has argued these direct estimates should be substituted for the usual commercial residual estimates of personal saving because of their superior quality. See also discussions of this point in Smyth [144], Dorrance [36, p. 207] and Friend [51, pp. 54–57].

and users of funds in the economy. The steadily increasing importance of financial institutions as a group was documented relative to national income, national assets, or wealth, although there was some evidence of retardation in the pace of this increasing intermediation going into the mid-fifties. The combined share of current net personal savings flows entrusted to them had increased from one-third before 1929 to well over half, even if consumer durables were included in saving. Considering only intangible assets, the share of their deposits had risen from about two-fifths to two-thirds. Long-term averages and cycles in the rates of growth (and shares) of each type of institution were examined, and while the concentration of resources within each type had generally been increasing, it "does not seem to be more pronounced than in other branches of the economy in which large enterprises play an important role" [54, p. 7].[30] These intermediaries had reduced the share of their assets supplied to business from two-fifths in 1929 to only one-fourth in 1952—corporate bonds and term loans declining from one-fifth of their assets in 1933 to one-tenth in 1952. Nevertheless, their share of all external funds absorbed by all other economic groups had progressively increased to well over half of the total; but "in normal periods (1900–29 and 1945–52) financial intermediaries have supplied approximately two-fifths of all external funds absorbed by nonfinancial corporations and approximately one-fourth of their total net financing (i.e., external financing plus internal net saving). The relative constancy of these proportions is perhaps the most significant finding of this part of the investigation." [54, p. 8.]

Goldsmith emphasized the absence at the time he was writing of a "much needed general theory of financial institutions." His chapter on "The Meaning of the (Major) Findings" largely involved factoring the percentage shares of intermediaries into the products of other ratios whose behavior is examined. For instance, he found that the past trends in the share of intermediaries in national assets were largely explained by movements in ratios of intangible to tangible assets, the ratio of "deadweight" government debt to national assets, and changes in asset prices. Much of this work is imaginative, all of it is descriptively interesting, and many of his "intermediate" or "explanatory" ratios are important objects of study in their own right. But adequate scientific explanation and understanding requires consistent estimates of the

[30] Also significantly, "the increase in concentration has not been unbroken, and . . . was more pronounced in the 1920's and during the Great Depression than before or after" (p. 87).

parameters of interacting sets of well specified and stochastic supply and demand equations that properly incorporate the full range of important asset and liability choices of each relevant, and relatively homogeneous, sector of the economy. The theoretical frameworks [31] and statistical methodology to make this possible were (largely) developed after Goldsmith's work.

Within a few more years [32] Goldsmith was able to round out the accounting framework of the economy by providing careful estimates of the national wealth and balance sheets [58] of the United States and its principal sectors, both for seven benchmark years running from 1900 to 1945, and annually thereafter through 1958. Estimates were developed on a net (depreciated) and a gross basis, both in constant (1947–49) prices and current (replacement) values. An important study of the effects of price level changes on net worth in national and sectoral balance sheets was included. Most of the general findings, however, again addressed themselves to shifts in the relative importance of different classes of real and intangible assets, and among assets and liabilities and income, both in national aggregates and within sectors. But these valuable historical perspectives are only the first fruits of this massive, well organized capital stock of knowledge. These extensive and carefully researched tables of data provided by Goldsmith and his associates, as they stand, will continue to provide important inputs to further research for years to come on the impact of financing and balance sheet adjustments on various types of current spending. As the usefulness and need for this kind of data becomes more fully apparent, the author's scholarly discussions of the process of preparing such estimates will also contribute to the work of extending their series of balance sheet and wealth data on a current basis, hopefully on an official basis by some government agency.[33]

[31] Notably modern theories of portfolio balance and capital market equilibrium (see references on pages) and stock-flow models of dynamic adjustment. In lamenting the lack of a general theory of financial institutions, Goldsmith in footnote [54, p. 15] remarks that the work of Gurley and Shaw [63] and [64] appeared after his manuscript was written, as did [57]. See also comments on this general problem in the concluding section of this paper.

[32] In this connection, mention should be made of Kuznets' early discussion (1938) of "The Measurement of National Wealth" [93]; Goldsmith's paper on "Measuring National Wealth in a System of Social Accounting" [57] and other papers in this volume.

[33] See also *Measuring the Nation's Wealth* by the Wealth Inventory Planning Study of George Washington University published as volume 29 in the National Bureau's Studies in Income and Wealth (1964).

IV. CAPITAL MARKETS AND INTEREST RATES

Braddock Hickman's studies of corporate bond financing [69] [70] [72] must surely rank as one of the classics in the entire literature on capital markets and corporation finance. The work was based on a detailed and exhaustive tabulation of over 28,000 straight railroad, utility, and industrial bonds outstanding at any time over the period 1900–43 [34] together with information on interest rates, defaults, losses, and investor experience. The first study to appear related the volume of issues, outstanding and extinguishments of corporate bonds to changes in corporate size, price levels, interest rates and conditions in the corporate markets, stages of the business cycle, and corporate liquidity, earnings and taxes. The complex strands of interrelation between each of the series are carefully sorted out for each stage of the business cycle, with an informal and penetrating discussion of the underlying forces that seem to best explain the behavior. The whole analysis is pregnant with insight and with suggested hypotheses for still further work—work which to this day is being facilitated by the total of 750 pages (including volume 3) of tables of well-organized primary data.

The second long study turned to the relation between bond quality and investor experience. Defaults averaged only 2.75 per cent of all outstandings through 1930 (but reached a peak of nearly 15 per cent by 1936, due largely to railroad issues), and over 94 per cent of all contractual interest was paid over the entire forty-four-year period. Capital losses on defaulted issues were offset however, by gains on called bonds (or 1944 prices on outstandings), so that all these bonds treated as one portfolio would have shown no loss and realized lifetime yields equaled offering yields. (If 1944 prices are out of the past, never to return, so is the Great Depression!)

Within the aggregates, the relation between investor experience and various measures of quality, assessed at time of issue, was analyzed in detail. *Default rates* rose almost uniformly with lower quality, whether quality was measured by agency ratings, acceptance on legal lists, market rating (issue yield spread over yield on highest grade concurrent issues), earnings coverage, size of issue, size of issuer and lien position. The errors in rating bonds were traced principally to the business cycle and to the difficulty of forecasting *industry* trends (within industry groups, relative rankings were much superior to the over-all good results). *Loss rates* were also greater on lower grade issues, but the risk

[34] All issues are for $5 million or more plus a sample of smaller issues.

premiums (extra promised yield on issue) *more* than compensated, so that life-span yields on low grades were higher than on higher grade issues. But the higher *average* returns for all holders for the entire period were associated with greater variability in realized returns over difficult subgroups of years *and* with greater dispersion in the performance within the lower grade groups within each subperiod of years studied. We may observe in passing that these and many other empirical results developed in this work accord well with the expectations generated by the theoretical models which have since been developed.

More recently Atkinson [3] has extended the record well into the postwar period, including convertible as well as nonconvertible bonds and private placements as well as public issues. Significantly, while the quality of new issues after the war was generally considerably higher than before, quality measures were generally deteriorating during the postwar period.

In the first postwar decade, residential mortgage debt grew by $80 billion—about twice the increase in either corporate bonds or consumer credit. Klaman [88] in his *Volume of Mortgage Debt in the Postwar Decade* developed the first good data on the fund flows in this important segment of the capital market. This was quickly followed by a study [87] tracing and analyzing the rapid *Postwar Rise of Mortgage Companies.* This was a new form of financial institution that rapidly developed a major role in the origination, and the distribution to large institutional investors, of government guaranteed residential mortgages. In a broader, comprehensive later study of *The Postwar Residential Mortgage Market* [86], he traced the institutionalization of the market, the growing role of its government guaranteed segment and the standardization of the mortgage instrument along modern lines even on conventional loans. Data on gross and net flows were further refined, and for the first time a series of interest rates for conventional loans was developed that has been taken over and developed further by government—and in commendable Bureau fashion, the data pointed up the need for much additional data. An up-to-date and comprehensive discussion of the mortgage portfolio policies of major institutional lenders was included, along with the development of the innovation of forward commitments. This new technique, between large lenders and large builders, had major effects on the time of fluctuations in residential building activity, and significantly changed the position of mortgages in the financial planning and portfolio policies of the major lenders.

Robinson [130] studied the postwar market for *State and Local*

Government Securities. He analyzed the demands for funds by the issuers and has an especially clear review of the marketing and secondary distribution of these securities. Although not developing a refined analysis of the portfolio considerations underlying the supply-of-funds functions for these securities, he was able through approximations to develop arithmetic estimates of the value of the tax-exemption subsidy they enjoy. Interestingly enough, his estimates indicated that the value of the subsidy to borrowing governments had been rapidly falling during the postwar period to the mid-fifties, and that an increasing share of the federal revenue loss was accruing to the investors rather than the issuers. Ott and Meltzer's later, more refined estimates confirmed the conclusion for 1960 data [125].

Saulnier, Halcrow and Jacoby prepared a comprehensive review of the nature and scope of federal credit activities and lending agencies [135] and assessed their wide ranging impacts both on financial markets and directly affected activities in housing, agriculture, etc. Wojnilower used bank examination records to study the *Quality of Bank Loans* [157], and Seiden studied the *Quality of Trade Credit* [139].

Meiselman and Shapiro [108] developed the very much more refined data that required careful statistical analysis of the sources and uses of funds for all nonfinancial corporations broken down into nine sector groups. Goldsmith [55] analyzed data on the flow of funds and balance sheets to develop a comprehensive summary of the major structural characteristics of the American capital market in the first decade and a half after the war, and the principal patterns in the shifts in holding and flows during that period. Although he found that changes in capital market techniques to that point ten years ago were less far-reaching than that of the 1920's or 1930's, he does point up sale and lease-back financing, and the increasing substitution of the professional management for security portfolios.

One of the major developments of the postwar period has been the rapid growth in size and importance of private pension plans. Cagan studied the *Effect of Pension Plans on Aggregate Saving* [15] on the basis of sample survey data. Using a well-developed theoretical framework and careful statistical procedures, he reached the important conclusion that most of the growth in pension funds increases national savings, since for the larger part neither employers' nor employees' contributions are substituted for other forms of personal savings. Holland projected the growth and portfolio composition of *Private Pension Funds* [75] and anticipated still more rapid growth of state and local funds with major impacts on the capital markets. Just two years ago, Roger Murray completed a summary volume on the *Economic Aspects of Pensions* [121], carefully developing their implications for total savings, for economic growth and stability, for major capital markets and other financial institutions, and assessed the issues raised for public policy.

The Bureau's recent work on interest rates has a long history going back to Macaulay's classic study of bond yields, interest rates, and stock prices [105] three decades ago. Quite apart from the tabulations of data going back to 1856 for most series (the data alone take up 300 pages), the study is noteworthy for its early careful development of the concept of long-term interest rates, which antedated other, now better known, work in important respects, including prior development of the concept of the "duration" of an income stream (which Hicks later termed the "average period of production" or "contango" [73]). Much of the very philosophical introduction is still of interest, though some is of course badly dated by now. The conceptualization and consideration of "economic drift" in the relation of bond yield to grades was pioneering and valuable, and the careful empirical tracing of leads and lags in the many series is still a useful source reference to patterns of historical behavior.

Hickman's unpublished 1942 manuscript on the *Term Structure of Interest Rates* [71] should also be mentioned because of its substantial influence in widespread informal circulation and its early critical analysis of the Lutz [104] and Hicks [73] theories of the links between long and short rates in the market place through "expectations" and arbitraging operations. Data were developed to compare realized holding period yields with the implicit forecasts of the yield curve, much in the manner of Culbertson [29] many years later.

Durand pioneered at about the same time with the development of his famous series on *Basic Yields of Corporate Bonds* [38] for 1900–42, which have been so extensively used as source data for later research. The series was refined and extended to 1947 in collaboration with Winn [39]. Shay studied two decades of new auto-financing rates [142], while Juster and Shay [83] studied the relation between finance rates charged on instalment credit and the demand for credit, thus developing a theoretical model for the analysis of borrowing decisions. Kessel [85] studied the *Cyclical Behavior of the Term Structure of Interest Rates,* building in part on the earlier work of Meiselman [109]. Kessel showed that liquidity premiums were also present in the data, and Cagan followed shortly with a careful study of *changes* in the cyclical behavior of the term structure [14].

The late Joseph Conard just four years ago gave a progress report on *The Behavior of Interest Rates* [20] summarizing the results obtained in analyses of rates in the mortgage market, direct placements (Cohan) [18], seasonal movements in short- and long-term issues, and the spreads between new and seasoned issues, as well as on the term structure itself. Just last year, in *Essays on Interest Rates* [66] substantial further analytical results were reported in most of these areas. Still more recently, Diller in [34] reports more refined, theoretical and empirical results on the term structure of rates viewed through the "window" of the "expectations hypothesis" combined with a sophisticated model of linear adaptive forecasting.

V. STRATEGY AND PRIORITIES FOR FURTHER FINANCIAL RESEARCH

As I indicated in the introduction to this paper, all this massive and valuable output of financial research from the Bureau over the last three decades or so represents the natural evolution in the hands of able scholars of the first Exploratory Committee's conception of a "new approach to (research in) finance" enunciated a generation ago. In such a context, an ex post judgment can surely be made that rarely has so wise and comprehensive a research program been developed and implemented so effectively.

The initial committee called for comprehensive surveys of our financial structure that would bring out the *interrelationships* between markets and institutions. In response, the Bureau pioneered in the development of the basic conceptual frameworks of the flow of funds, national balance sheet, and national wealth accounts that are essential complements to their earlier development of national income accounts for everyone concerned with the study of financial markets and the mutual interaction of finance with spending on real goods and services. The new accounting frameworks would have remained elegant and suggestive architect's drawings of nests of more "empty boxes" (in Clapham's earlier phrase) without the Bureau's patient, persistent, systematic and often very imaginative work to grub out and incorporate the hard data (and some that is not so solid, through no fault of their own) required to give real empirical substance to these abstract conceptual frameworks of national and social accounting.

The Exploratory Committee a generation ago called for research to provide *perspective*—and the work of Kuznets and his associates in the series on capital formation and its financing, and much of Goldsmith's work on savings, intermediaries and balance sheets have provided a fuller, more detailed, and more extended historical perspective on secular trends, long cycles and major shifts in the structure of these basic data than anyone but they would have thought possible.

The early committee noted the pervasive lack of knowledge at the time regarding the markets for major types of credits, notably consumer instalment debt, business finance of all types other than traditional short-term bank loans and mortgages. The studies in the Bureau's initial program of financial research over a period of years made a quantum advance in our knowledge of the users and suppliers and the volume of each of these major types of credit in the economy. In addition, valuable monographs were produced on important, newly emerging types of financing such as term loans with regular amortization for business firms. Investor's returns and losses on nearly a half century's issues of corporate bonds, and their experience with major classes of mortgage loans, were carefully studied. It is also noteworthy that many of these earlier studies made important contributions to our knowledge specifically by developing very revealing cross-sectional profiles of the reliance on different types of financing by different income, demographic, industry, and size-of-firm breakdowns *within* the sectors usually specified in the flow-of-funds accounts. Also, quite significantly, many of the earlier as well as later studies developed at least first order explanations in a true scientific sense which modeled the observed cross-sectional and time series patterns of financial behavior.

As the program of financial research at the Bureau evolved, the results and insights of earlier projects and new developments in the marketplace indicated the need for further studies on a more current and detailed basis for particular types of credits and sectors previously studied, notably mortgages and the growing panoply of government lending and loan guarantees. In the context of the growing body of organized knowledge produced by earlier studies at the Bureau and elsewhere, it was natural that the recommendations of the Exploratory Committees in 1954 and again in 1964 should focus somewhat more specifically on further research needed on securities and capital markets. In line with these suggestions, several studies of changes in the quality of different types of credit and changing yields and patterns of interest rates have been completed, and considerable further work is under way on interest rates. Other studies have been completed on markets for state and local securities, shifting flows of capital funds in the postwar economy and the growth and significance of pension funds.

The impressive mass of well-organized substantive knowledge produced by this program of *Research on Finance and Capital Markets* as it has evolved over the last three decades or so has clearly justified the high priority the Bureau has given it in the allocation of its over-all resources and research effort, and the confidence of those providing special grants for major parts of this work. Knowledge of our financial structure and institutions has grown in cumulative fashion, not only within the Bureau's own program, but still more broadly as others have carried on and extended the economic accounting work started at the Bureau, and as other scholars have used Bureau data and results as essential inputs to their own further studies. Beyond the scholarly community, the fruits of this research have contributed in a very significant way to the background of knowledge and understanding of a much wider audience of policy makers and "practical" people whose decisions directly affect the numbers that we find in our national balance sheets, flows-of-funds statements and national income accounts.

As the Bureau plans the financial research to undertake in at least the earlier part of its second half-century, I see no need for any sharp break in the main lines of development we have traced in its ongoing program. The Bureau's financial research staff has developed special expertise in certain types of fundamental substantive research that is a very valuable asset. In planning its future financial research, the Bureau should give full weight to these comparative advantages and allow for the relative efficiency that comes from the momentum of a continuing program. Many of the studies the Bureau should undertake are quite natural extensions of the evolution of its earlier work, and its traditional expertise will make an essential contribution to most of the others. The studies required to gain a better understanding of the shifting patterns of allocations of funds in our financial markets, for instance, will require more complete information on gross as well as net flows in the flow-of-funds accounts, more detailed information on both the balance sheets and financial flows for more homogeneous subgroups within the present sectors, a better matching of interest rates and other financial prices to existing data, and so on. Rapid changes have been occurring in the structure and operations of many of our major financial institutions and major financial markets, as well as in the types of instruments used in financing nonresidential construction and other important types of investment. Just as the Bureau studied the emerging term loan and new patterns of financing inventories and receivables in the early days of its financial research program, there is now need, for instance, for systematic and comprehensive studies of the commercial paper market as a third banking system, of the leasing of industrial equipment, and, perhaps within a few years as the procedures mature, the private placement market for new issues of common stock.

But, while appropriately preserving momentum and continuity, the *pace* of evolutionary change in the Bureau's financial research program needs to be stepped up to meet the needs of new circumstances and newly pressing issues, which I will discuss specifically just below. Effective response to these needs and opportunities will require that new projects be undertaken with a substantially different balance of immediate research objectives and a rather different mix of research methodologies than has been typical of the Bureau's financial research in the past. Such an effective response to these needs will also require that new dimensions and approaches be added to some of its other, more traditional types of projects.

Conditions have changed in fundamental ways which considerably alter the marginal social values of the different types of financial research the Bureau might now undertake. The first change largely reflects major achievements of the Bureau's own earlier efforts. We have applauded the impressive degree to which the pervasive lack of knowledge of our financial structure lamented in earlier years has been displaced by masses of well-organized financial data and other factually descriptive information on its operations, including major trends in its historical development. We also noted with approval that even some of the earlier as well as later studies also developed "at least first order explanations in a true scientific sense" of some of the observed patterns of financial behavior, and that somewhat more powerful or sophisticated analytical methods are being used in more recent work, especially on studies of certain aspects of interest rates. We also noted that in many other cases an informed and careful organization of data had uncovered apparently important empirical patterns of covariation and features of behavior that would have to be explained by subsequent research.

In this context it seems clear that in planning its future financial research the Bureau should now begin to give a considerably higher priority to developing a more probative *analysis* and *scientific explanation* of existing factual knowledge, including knowledge of first order relationships within the data. This shift in priorities is an important one, even though more detailed breakdowns of existing data and other new information will often be required *as one part of the further research* needed to develop a more adequate scientific analysis of the issues posed by factual knowledge already available from earlier research.

To over-simplify a little, priorities are now properly shifted from the necessary first stage of determining *what,* for instance, the major descriptive historical trends have been to quite heavy emphasis on developing well-specified and behaviorally-motivated structural explanations of *why* they have been so, precisely in order to develop a much firmer basis for assessing the probable persistence or change in these trends in the future—the *so whats* that enter into public and private decisions. Similarly, with the structure of the flows-of-funds accounts worked out and numbers in each of the cells over a considerable period on a quarterly and annual basis, the primary objective of further research moves to the development and testing of alternative scientific explanations or models of the multivariate, stochastic, and simultaneous relationships between the various numbers in the tables (other than accounting identities), taking appropriate account of other relevant data such as interest rates, incomes, and balance sheet positions. As already suggested as a general proposition, in both these illustrative cases, the odds are high that this other-directed research will require very substantial amounts of data not yet tabulated or estimated, but the accumulation of additional data will be incident to, and determined by, the *analytical specification* of the primary research objectives which lie elsewhere.

The second change in conditions that alters the marginal social productivity of different types of financial research for the Bureau may quite properly be characterized as the technological change that has shifted the production function for research itself. This technological change in turn reflects the combined and interacting effects of major developments in the relevant economic theory and in the sophistication and power of the available techniques of statistical analysis and testing. It also, of course, involves the quite remarkable improvements we have seen in the capacity, speed, and efficiency of computers, since vast amounts of numerical calculation are required by empirical work designed to use modern statistical methods to choose among alternative specifications of sophisticated economic models and obtain good estimates of their structural parameters and other statistical properties. Although modern computers greatly facilitate record-keeping and data accumulation, their comparative advantage is generally even greater in scientific work of the kind just described.

Taken together, these three mutually reinforcing developments have opened up frontiers of scientific analysis in our areas of interest that were out of the question just a relatively few years ago. Equally important, they probably have reduced the relative costs of a given quantum and quality of research directed to scientific explanation and analysis quite substantially in comparison with the costs of a given quantum and quality of research to add to our stock of financial data (except as by-products of established reporting systems) and other factually descriptive information. *Either* the "new product" or the "relative cost" effect of this three-fold technological change, by itself, would justify a considerable shift in the emphasis of the Bureau's financial research program from the balance typical of earlier, and even relatively recent, years. Taken together, a still more substantial shift toward scientific analysis is indicated.

Consider for a moment that the text of Goldsmith's *Financial Intermediaries* was written before the theoretical work of Gurley and Shaw on the financial aspects of economic development [63], [64], and [65] appeared, and well before the subsequent studies stimulated by their theoretical effort that led to substantial modifications of their initial models. In particular, most of Tobin's classic work [148], [150], [151] on these matters has appeared within the last decade. Consider also that Markowitz' initial paper [106]—which for the first time explained the diversification of asset holdings by investors in the context of a rational and operational economic model—appeared at about the same time as Copeland's *Moneyflows,* and the monograph [107] giving the full body of his analysis appeared much later. Most of the resulting theory of the optimal choices among different mixtures of assets and liabilities and scale of operations by *financial intermediaries* (given their assessments of returns and risks and degree of risk aversion) has been developed *within the last five years* in the work of Cootner [26], [27], Lintner [102, section II and III], Houthakker [78], and Pyle [128]. Similarly, systematic studies at a theoretical level of the *interactions* between the conditionally optimal portfolios of individual investors and intermediaries in even idealized purely competitive securities markets, and the properties of the resulting set of equilibrium prices in such markets, have also only been available in the last half decade (see Sharpe [141], Lintner [95], [102], Fama [48], [49], and Mossin [119], [120]). Indeed, a systematic analysis of the equilibrium of securities markets when there is no riskless security, when investors have *different* assessments about everything, and when many of them can't or won't sell short and also hold only limited numbers of stocks in their portfolios, has appeared only in the last twelve months (Lintner [95]). On another important dimension, it is again largely in recent years that models of the stochastic dynamics of stock price over time under idealized conditions (shades of martingales and random walks!) have been developed (see Cootner [27] and Fama [47]). Moreover, models of the optimal adjustment of individual portfolios over time, with explicit allowance for transactions costs and other constraints on perfect fluidity, and based on the investor's own unique judgments of future prospects, have been developed only quite recently in the work of Smith [143] and Pogue [127].

These rather substantial bodies of theoretical work bear directly on the concerns of the Bureau's own program of financial research. They could not be used to help formulate the statistical analysis in most of the work we have reviewed because they did not yet exist. While substantial further work will be required to modify, develop, and adapt these theoretical frameworks to many of the situations that will be found in practice, they do appear to have reached a stage of development where they can be very useful in much of the Bureau's further empirical work. As already indicated, these efforts will also be able to draw on a rapidly growing and equally important body of knowledge of statistical procedures. To cite just a pair of illustrative examples, econometricians today are in a much better position than they were even a decade or so ago to get good, unbiased estimates of the separate parameters and reaction coefficients that appear in a context of *mutual interdependence* and feedback, and in a context of dynamic sequences of adjustments over time. As one more situation which is important for financial research, econometricians are also in a much better position to analyze just what is going on when there is reason to believe that decisions are really being made on the basis of some sort of normalized figures (for current earnings, for instance) rather than, or in addition to, the publicly published figures that reflect a variety of essentially random and transient phenomena. Once again, these and other developments in statistical technique are not foolproof, but while they provide no complete insurance against misleading inferences, they do greatly improve the quality of the work in many important situations which arise frequently.

To this point we have been examining the shifts in emphasis that seem to be desirable, as the Bureau plans its future financial research program, in view of the stock of financial knowledge already built up from past research efforts, and the changing environment of research methodology. We now turn to some major issues of primary public concern that have a direct bearing on the *needs* for different kinds of financial research.

Consider first the implications of our national commitments to maintaining high levels of employment and growth *and* reasonable price stability. Postwar experience confirms our belief that the massive fluctuations in over-all economic activity and employment which characterized major business cycles in the past can be effectively prevented. But what used to be called minor cycles of alternating irregular sequences of under- and over-utilization of our real resources continue. Periods of excessive demands and accelerating increases in prices have distorted allocations of resources and financial markets, while efforts to dampen the economy and bring inflation under control have seriously exacerbated the distortions in every case in both respects. As our national aspirations rise to the minimization of what some economists at the Bureau now call "growth recessions," what can financial research contribute to the knowledge required simultaneously to satisfy our goal of price stability?

The fundamental answer is that a better understanding of the operations of financial markets and of the interdependencies between them, as well as a better understanding of the impact of financial considerations on spending decisions throughout the economy, can make major contributions to the development of better fiscal as well as monetary policy. Fiscal policy can ignore these financial considerations *only if* all spending decisions can be fully explained by incomes, real stocks of goods and rates of output. No responsible economist even acts as if he believes that anymore. Similarly, the design of appropriate monetary policy must take this vast network of financial relationships and impacts into account *unless total* spending is all that matters *and* the level, or rate of change, of some controllable monetary aggregate determines total spending without outside help or significant influence—and apart from perhaps a few zealots given to oversimplification, no one even acts as if he believes *either* of these propositions anymore. But those who attach primary importance to money as such have been unable to delineate clearly and operationally the channels through which its effects spread themselves out over the economy, nor the interactions of monetary policy with fiscal policy and other real, financial, and structural phenomena which, it is agreed, also influence the course of events to at least some significant extent. At the same time, along with their more traditional concerns, all modern neo- and post-neo-Keynesians attach very great significance to both monetary and financial considerations as well—and are working hard to learn more about them.

This growing concern is clearly reflected in the development of their econometric models for forecasting the level and structure of the gross national product. Indeed it seems clear that, along with the use of more refined statistical procedures and careful specification of the dynamic stock-flow adjustment processes in individual sectors, much of the credit for the very real improvements we have observed in the forecasting record of econometric models over the last two decades must be attributed to the increasing attention that has been given to financial considerations in the formulation of the models. While the forecasting record of even the more recent and sophisticated models still leaves a great deal to be desired, as Zarnowitz' recent reviews [159], [160], [161] clearly demonstrate, very substantial progress has been made. The contributions that fuller and more careful attention to financial considerations have made to this progress, strongly suggest the importance of fuller development along these lines.

To get a quick perspective, we should recall that Klein's pioneering effort published two decades ago [89] was concerned with monetary matters only to the extent of fitting a Keynesian liquidity preference function to determining "the" corporate interest rate and holdings of "active" and "idle" cash balances simultaneously with the rest of the system, given excess reserves, but the interest rate affected demand only in the equation for rental housing. In another decade, a massive joint committee of no less than twenty-five economists, working under the sponsorship of the Brookings Institution and the Social Science Research Council [37], developed a much more advanced model of production and demands for output that among other improvements included a broader range of financial impacts on spending.[35] Of particular interest here as part of the over-all project, Frank de Leeuw of the research staff at the Board of Governors of the Federal Reserve System contributed a nineteen-simultaneous-equation model of the interactions of seven financial sectors [37], although only short and long interest rates and cash balances entered directly into the rest of the system. De Leeuw's work was continued with Gramlich and developed into the

[35] Not only did interest rates enter into the equations for each type of fixed investment but, interestingly enough, cash balances entered as one determinant of consumer demand.

financial sector of the joint MIT-FRB model with Modigliani, Ando, Rasche, Shapiro, and others [32], [31], [129], and [113].

This MIT-FRB model includes the fullest treatment of the financial sector in any of the available econometric models of the economy.[36] Most earlier models of this type had effectively assumed that monetary considerations had their effects on spending entirely through their effects upon interest rates, both as costs of new financing and as opportunity costs of holding durable goods. In the present model, this channel is implemented by calculating different costs of capital for several different types of investment; for single and for multiple-family housing, business plant, producer equipment, state and local construction, and for consumer durable goods. In addition, consumption expenditures are very significantly affected by consumers' wealth (net worth) and hence the value of equities, which by way of dividend yields depend in a complex way on corporate bond yields and rates of inflation. Finally, monetary factors affect the economy through credit rationing in the housing market.

By introducing these two additional channels, and developing the first in much greater detail than previously attempted, this model finds much stronger monetary and financial effects on economic activity than had been shown in earlier efforts of this type. But, though large and strong after a considerable time has elapsed, the effects of a one-billion dollar step increase in unborrowed reserves, for instance, builds only gradually, being half again as large on money GNP in the second calendar year following the increase as in the first, and still about as large in the third. Even in real terms, the delayed effects in the second year following the monetary change are about as large as those in the first, but are reversed over the long run. Quite significantly and plausibly, all these effects of monetary policy are smaller if the action is taken when there is slack in the economy and divided yields are higher, than when the economy is taut and the equity market is high; but simulations with this model show that under both taut and slack initial conditions, the effects of monetary action build much more slowly to their peak levels than do the effects of tax changes, and these in turn build less rapidly than changes in public spending. See [31].

This model clearly demonstrates the progress that has so far been

[36] In connection with the increasing interest of non-Chicago economists in monetary influences, we may note that the more recent Evans-Klein-Wharton [41] and O.B.E. [94] models also include fuller financial sectors than earlier Keynesian treatments, but still in a much more rudimentary form than the MIT-FRB model.

made in incorporating a structure of financial elements into GNP forecasting models and the substantial gains that can follow from such efforts. Also, because this is the most complete and sophisticated formal model of the financial structure of the economy and its interaction with real phenomena yet available, it provides a convenient framework in which to raise a variety of important issues for further financial research whose resolution can contribute in a very significant way to a better understanding of the inflationary consequences of alternative high employment policies and, more generally, in choosing among alternative mixtures of fiscal and monetary policies. In making these observations, I am, of course, not suggesting that the Bureau's financial research program should undertake to develop full GNP models itself, but rather than many of the critical issues and further improvements needed in such over-all models depend in an essential way upon a substantial program of *financial research as such.*

The core of the eighteen-equation-financial block of the MIT-FRB model is a set of interrelated stock-flow adjustment relations involving bank demands for free reserves and nonbank demands for deposits and currency that absorb required reserves.[37] Unborrowed reserves and the discount rate act as external or exogenous elements that affect the bill rate and the commercial paper rate with essentially short lags through these core relations. But the corporate bond rate depends on the commercial paper rate in a term structure equation with a long distributed lag, which gives less weight to the current quarter's CP rate than to its average value in the fourth through ninth preceding quarters. *All* other interest rates affecting demands for funds from *all* branches of the capital market are then based on this corporate rate with some additional lags. These other long interest rates then affect the relevant costs of capital, which affect spending on capital goods with further long lags. Additionally, all the important wealth effects on consumer spending come from shifts in dividend yields on equities that are estimated with a five-quarter lag on the corporate bond rate (with three-fifths of the total weight on the second and earlier quarters).

The surprisingly delayed effects that the model ascribes to mone-

[37] All these comments are based on the latest published version of the model as of May 1969 [31]. Internal FRB staff working with the model may well have allowed for many of the comments made here, at least in an informal way. It should also be clear that the purpose of these observations on the MIT-FRB model is to show the need for the strategy of further financial research I am recommending for the Bureau, rather than to critique the existing model.

tary policy, even though the total effect is large, clearly come from this pyramided structure of lags on long lags outside the money market itself, together with its failure to allow for possible additional channels of impact, and its allowance for rationing effects only in the housing sector. But suppose for the moment that the corporate rate is properly explained and that the lags of investment spending from costs of capital have also been correctly estimated. *If,* for instance, further research should show that dividend yields depend significantly on bill rates as well as corporate bond rates (inflationary expectations being the same), then the important wealth effects on consumer spending would show up much more quickly than now estimated, and monetary policy would be regarded as a more effective instrument of shorter-run stabilization policy than is indicated by the evidence of the present model (though, even so, the total long-run effect might be less than presently indicated).

Similar judgments would of course follow if other more direct channels of monetary effects are actually present *and* operate with shorter lags, or if there are in fact significant rationing effects outside the housing market. In this connection, we note that costs of capital are estimated in each sector on the assumption that additional supplies of funds will be available at existing market rates, with no allowance for increasing costs of debt money as debt ratios rise or as earnings coverage falls,[38] nor for any rationing imposed by lenders when existing debt is regarded as excessive. Similarly, bank demands for free reserves are estimated on the basis of discount and bill rates in an appropriate type of stock-flow adjustment relation, but with no allowance for the rationing of 6 per cent money at "the window," during 1969 and 1970, even when rates on alternative federal, C.P., and Euro-dollar funds ranged from 8 per cent up to 12 per cent or so.

Some of the further research suggested by these questions regarding the existence and importance of credit rationing outside the housing market, and the identity and strength of possible additional linkages between different rates and markets, can doubtless be carried through by more statistical analysis of existing data or new data that is tabulated especially for the purpose—especially to provide data for more homogeneous subgroups of economic data.[39] Some of the studies can

[38] For some theory and evidence that at least indicate the need for further investigation—which is the essential point of all these comments—see, for instance, [96].

[39] For instance, the portfolio adjustment equations used in existing models explain the volume of savings in savings banks, savings and loan, and consumer time deposits, for instance, by relative interest rates (along with aggregate, net

safely proceed directly to the statistical testing and fitting of models formulated on the basis of general existing knowledge; [40] but in many others, important missing insights are likely to be obtained by careful field work with the men who are actually making the decisions in question.[41] Some of the studies will also need to give special attention to developing and analyzing information on the industrial organization of their market sectors, in order to properly incorporate the consequences of mutual interdependencies *within* markets that may substantially alter the relations *between* markets. Even though we know that rationing can occur within purely competitive markets [74], [112], matters of industrial structure are undoubtedly important in many practical instances.

A substantially different set of issues is raised by the tie between the short-term interest rate (bill or commercial paper) and the rate on long bonds. It is quite clear that long rates do not fluctuate as widely as short rates, but the exact form of the relation between them is still a rather murky question. The models in current use and favor allow for the effect of arbitrage between different maturities of like securities,

worth, and income). Thompson's earlier work [146] however, showed that a breakdown by income into a group not using market alternatives, and another more sophisticated group who were making comparisons between securities and deposits, was a very important factor in the allocation of total personal financial savings among institutions. The interest elasticities now computed cannot be expected to be stable over time, as income distributions and awareness of market alternatives change. Another important breakdown of data which is needed to analyze the allocations of personal savings of course involves the separation of data for owners of unincorporated businesses and data on personal trust accounts, on which some work is now being done [56].

As another illustration, a single equation is used to estimate the public's demand for demand deposits without separately allowing for the shifting mix between corporations and consumers, or variations in compensating balance requirements. Similarly, although the present model has allowed for the substantial differences in the factors determining investment outlays for plant as distinct from equipment, a single corporate aggregate for each is used without separating industrials from utilities and other groupings, which should be studied separately.

[40] Kresge's study of commercial bank call reports currently underway at the Bureau is one good illustration.

[41] Two different interest rates clearly do not belong in the same *structural* equation when they do not enter into the choices being made by any significant group of decision makers. By the same token, such investigations and study of the actual decision-making processes in the field are likely to provide new insights into the existence and form of additional structural linkages which have not been incorporated to date.

which in a market equilibrium would imply that the *expected* long rate at any time is a compound average of expectations regarding future short rates. We noted above the valuable recent study of Diller at the Bureau on interest rate structures in this context when future short rates are assumed to be estimated with what are technically known as linear adaptive forecasting procedures which seem to match the observed data relatively well. These procedures are regressive in the sense that they allow for investors' expectations that current rates will gradually return to some more normal long-run level, but they do not allow for the additional possibility that investors also to some extent tend to extrapolate recent shorter-run trends in interest rate changes. But when this additional and very reasonable type of expectation is introduced along with the other, the statistical analysis becomes considerably more complicated than in the models carefully analyzed so far.

Further complications are introduced by efforts to allow at the same time for the fact that investors and borrowers are concerned with inflation. Irving Fisher as early as 1896 had shown that in markets of rational men, nominal (quoted) interest rates should compensate for *expected* rates of inflation, as well as the deflated returns that will clear the market in real terms on the basis of over-all supply and demand considerations. Still further complications are again introduced by the fact that it seems reasonable to assume that people tend to think that recent price trends will persist for some time into the future, even while they also expect that rates of inflation will gradually recede to more normal levels—and this still further complicates the statistical work because complex weighted averages of past price movements and of earlier interest rates *must* both be estimated simultaneously.

While past experience unquestionably does condition judgments concerning probable future movements in prices and interest rates, one is surely uneasy about the present state of our knowledge of *how* these effects work themselves out in practice, and a substantial program of further research is clearly going to be required on this set of problems. At this time, we need only observe that substantially different average lags and time profiles have been found when data covering different periods were used. But while the available estimates of average lags have varied to a disturbing degree, the fact that they are all relatively long raises the further troublesome possibility that they may be serving in part as proxies for some Kuznets-Burns long-cycle or trend effect on other variables.[42] Moreover, the models simply assume that inflationary expectations build up and dampen out on *the same time profile* of past price changes. There is some reason to believe that behavior during a period (such as, hopefully, the present) when the pace of inflation is being reduced may be more favorable than the present models would indicate.

All the problems and uncertainties, of course, arise fundamentally from the fact that neither expectations of future short-term interest rates nor expectations of future rates of price inflation are directly observed and reported in the available data. Along with further testing and more refined analysis by statistical procedures of the data in hand, including the exploration of additional models,[43] it might be fruitful to develop a research team of economists and psychologists who would systematically study the actual formation of expectations by field interview, controlled experiment, or other appropriate means. The possibility of arranging for a group of banks and other institutions to keep a running record of their dated expectations of interest rates and rates of inflation six months ahead might also develop into a valuable source of data on explicit expectations for further statistical analysis.[44]

Apart from questions of other channels, rationing outside residential mortgage markets, and difficulties with estimating lag patterns, we can also observe that, like all other such models, the MIT-FRB model is still simply Keynesian in relying entirely on only one direct link between short and long interest rates. All its capital markets *as a group* are then cleared by the savings-equals-investment, ex post accounting identity. Strictly empirical nonstructural equations relate different long rates to each other. In particular, there is nothing on the supply and demand structure of the interrelationships *between* markets for long municipals, governments, agencies, utilities, industrials—nor on structural determinants of yield spreads between quality grades of corporates. Whether or not such detail proves to be important to the

[42] Interest rates have of course been on an essentially rising trend for nearly two decades, and the fits have been to this period. A question may also be raised regarding the number of degrees of freedom left after the data have been used to select the best length and degree of polynomial in the Almon [2] technique.

[43] For instance, the weights on the extrapolative and regressive expectations components are held fixed in present fitting procedures. These may well turn out to be a function of the sign and size of surprises, just as the response coefficients in early inventory models turned out to be a function of new orders and backlogs.

[44] Cooperating firms would of course be anonymous, as in Zarnowitz' and Juster's work.

construction of improved over-all global models for general economic forecasting and policy formulation (as MIT-FRB is designed to be)—and I am not alone in thinking it will be important in this broader context—this is clearly a matter of crucial importance to our own subject of finance and capital markets!

To meet these needs, however, further research will have to build up a much greater store of detailed institutional knowledge than we now have, and it will *also* have to fill in and build our knowledge of *how portfolio choices are made* by every major investor group in every market. We know that these portfolio choices involve judgments of *risks* as well as judgments of what will probably happen (expectations)—and in a portfolio context, they involve assessments of the *interdependencies of risks.*[45]

In planning its financial research program for the next decade or so, the Bureau could thus well take the development of the knowledge needed for a complete econometric model of the flow-of-funds accounts as one of its *ultimate* objectives of its over-all program. But, as the previous discussion should make clear, I am convinced that this ultimate objective itself requires a rather long series of individual studies that together will build up the more detailed knowledge of particular markets and of the portfolio choices of major investors influencing interactions within various clusters and subclusters of markets, which are necessary building blocks for such a large structure. Along with all these efforts, longer-term perspectives should be filled out and re-examined in the light of new data and more recent developments. In addition, although not specifically repeated here, many of the studies recommended by the 1964 review committee have not yet been implemented and should be included in the Bureau's planning if not being undertaken elsewhere before the Bureau gets to them.

The Bureau's work as it has accumulated and evolved over the last three decades has made a tremendous contribution to our stock of relevant, tested, and substantive knowledge of finance and capital markets. As it maintains the momentum of its program and adapts its effort to the issues and opportunities emerging for the seventies and eighties and beyond, its record of achievement and contribution the growing body of knowledge will surely be no less substantial.

[45] The portfolio balance equations in present models need only include the yields on the alternative assets, because they have to do with allocations of funds between (riskless) savings accounts or bills or cash. But when choices are between alternative risk assets, risk assessments as well as expected values are essential.

REFERENCES

[1] Alexander, Sidney S. "Changes in the Financial Structure of American Business Enterprise, 1900–40." Unpublished manuscript. New York: National Bureau of Economic Research.

[2] Almon, Shirley. "The Distributed Lag Between Capital Appropriations and Expenditures." *Econometrica* (January 1965).

[3] Atkinson, Thomas R., assisted by Elizabeth T. Simpson. *Trends in Corporate Bond Quality*. New York: National Bureau of Economic Research, 1967.

[4] Baumol, William J. "The Transactions Demand for Cash: An Inventory Theoretic Approach." *Quarterly Journal of Economics* (November 1952).

[5] Behrens, Carl F. *Commercial Bank Activities in Urban Mortgage Financing*. New York: National Bureau of Economic Research, 1952.

[6] Bernstein, Blanche. *The Pattern of Consumer Debt, 1935–36: A Statistical Analysis*. New York: National Bureau of Economic Research, 1940.

[7] Board of Governors of the Federal Reserve System. *Flow of Funds Accounts, 1945–1968*. Washington: Board of Governors of the Federal Reserve System, 1970.

[8] ———. "Flow of Funds Seasonally Adjusted." *Federal Reserve Bulletin* (November 1962).

[9] ———. "Revision of the Flow of Funds Accounts." *Federal Reserve Bulletin* (November 1965).

[10] Borts, George. "Review of Ulmer's Capital in Transportation." *American Economic Review* (December 1960).

[11] Brittain, John A. *Corporate Demand Policy*. Washington: Brookings Institution, 1966.

[12] Brunner, K., and Meltzer, A. H. "Predicting Velocity: Its Implications for Theory and Policy." *Journal of Finance* (May 1963).

[13] Burns, Arthur F., and Mitchell, Wesley C. *Measuring Business Cycles*. New York: National Bureau of Economic Research, 1946.

[14] Cagan, Phillip. *Changes in the Cyclical Behavior of Interest Rates*. New York: National Bureau of Economic Research, 1966.

[15] ———. *The Effect of Pension Plans on Aggregate Saving: Evidence from a Sample Survey*. New York: National Bureau of Economic Research, 1965.

[16] Chapman, John M., and associates. *Commercial Banks and Consumer Instalment Credit*. New York: National Bureau of Economic Research, 1940.

[17] Chudson, Walter A. *The Pattern of Corporate Financial Structure: A Cross-Section View of Manufacturing Mining, Trade and Construction, 1937*. New York: National Bureau of Economic Research, 1945.

[18] Cohan, Avery B. *Yields on Corporate Debt Directly Placed*. New York: National Bureau of Economic Research, 1967.

[19] Colean, Miles L. *The Impact of Government on Real Estate Finance in the United States*. New York: National Bureau of Economic Research, 1950.

[20] Conard, Joseph W. *The Behavior of Interest Rates: A Progress Report*. New York: National Bureau of Economic Research, 1966.

[21] Copeland, Morris A. "Consolidated Balance Sheet for the Banking Sector." *Journal of Political Economy* (1932).

[22] ———. *Proposal for a Revised Set of Summary Accounts and Supporting Financial Details*. Studies in Income and Wealth, Volume 22. Princeton: Princeton University Press for National Bureau of Economic Research, 1958.

[23] ———. "Seasonal Problems in Financial Administration." *Journal of Political Economy* (1920).

[24] ———. *A Study of Moneyflows in the United States.* New York: National Bureau of Economic Research, 1952.

[25] Coppock, Joseph D. *Government Agencies of Consumer Instalment Credit.* New York: National Bureau of Economic Research, 1940.

[26] Cootner, Paul. "The Liquidity of the Savings and Loan Industry." *Study of the Savings and Loan Industry.* Washington: Home Loan Bank Board, 1969.

[27] ———, ed. *The Random Character of Stock Market Prices.* Boston: MIT Press, 1964.

[28] Creamer, Daniel; Dobrovolsky, Sergei; and Borenstein, Israel. *Capital in Manufacturing and Mining: Its Formation and Financing.* Princeton: Princeton University Press for National Bureau of Economic Research, 1960.

[29] Culbertson, John M. "The Term Structure of Interest Rates." *Quarterly Journal of Economics* (November 1957).

[30] Dauer, Ernst A. *Comparative Operating Experience of Consumer Instalment Financing Agencies and Commercial Banks, 1929–41.* New York: National Bureau of Economic Research, 1944.

[31] de Leeuw, Frank, and Gramlich, Edward M. "The Channels of Monetary Policy." *Journal of Finance* (May 1969).

[32] ———. "The Federal Reserve-MIT Econometric Model." *Federal Reserve Bulletin* (January 1968).

[33] Diesslin, Howard G. *Agricultural Equipment Financing.* New York: National Bureau of Economic Research, 1955.

[34] Diller, Stanley. *The Seasonal Variation in Interest Rates.* New York: National Bureau of Economic Research, 1970.

[35] Dobrovolsky, Sergei P. *Corporate Income Retention, 1915–43.* New York: National Bureau of Economic Research, 1951.

[36] Dorrance, Graeme S. "Financial Accounting: Its Present State and Prospects." *Staff Papers,* International Monetary Fund (1966).

[37] Duesenberry, James S., *et al. Brookings Quarterly Econometric Model of the United States.* Chicago: Rand McNally, 1965.

[38] Durand, David. *Basic Yields of Corporate Bonds, 1900–1942.* New York: National Bureau of Economic Research, 1942.

[39] ———, and Winn, Willis J. *Basic Yields of Bonds, 1926–1947: Their Measurement and Pattern.* New York: National Bureau of Economic Research, 1947.

[40] ———. *Risk Elements in Consumer Instalment Financing.* New York: National Bureau of Economic Research, 1940.

[41] Evans, Michael K., and Klein, Lawrence R. *The Wharton Econometric Forecasting Model.* Philadelphia: Economics Research Unit, University of Pennsylvania, 1967.

[42] Exploratory Committee. *A Program of Financial Research,* Volume 1. New York: National Bureau of Economic Research, 1937.

[43] ———. *Research in the Capital Markets.* New York: National Bureau of Economic Research, 1964.

[44] ———. *Research in the Capital and Securities Markets.* New York: National Bureau of Economic Research, 1954.

[45] ———. *Research in the Securities Markets.* New York: National Bureau of Economic Research, 1946.

[46] Fama, Eugene F., and Babiak, Harvey. "Dividend Policy: An Empirical Analysis." *Journal of the American Statistical Association* (December 1968).
[47] ———. "Efficient Capital Markets: A Review of Theory and Empirical Work." *Journal of Finance* (May 1970).
[48] ———. "Risk, Return and Equilibrium." *Journal of Political Economy* (January-February 1971).
[49] ———. "Risk, Return and Equilibrium: Some Clarifying Comments." *Journal of Finance* (March 1968).
[50] Fisher, Ernest M. *Urban Real Estate Markets: Characteristics and Financing.* New York: National Bureau of Economic Research, 1951.
[51] Friend, Irwin, assisted by Vito Natrella. *Individuals' Saving.* New York: John Wiley and Sons, 1954.
[52] Goldsmith, Raymond W. *The Changing Structure of American Banking.* London: Routledge, 1933.
[53] ———. *Das deutsche grossbankkapital in seiner neueren entwicklung.* Berlin: Ebering, 1928.
[54] ———. *Financial Intermediaries in the American Economy since 1900.* Princeton: Princeton University Press for National Bureau of Economic Research, 1958.
[55] ———. *The Flow of Capital Funds in the Postwar Economy.* New York: National Bureau of Economic Research, 1965.
[56] ———. "Institutional Investors and the Stock Market." *50th Annual Report.* New York: National Bureau of Economic Research, 1970.
[57] ———. *Measuring National Wealth in a System of Social Accounting.* Studies in Income and Wealth, Volume 12. New York: National Bureau of Economic Research, 1950.
[58] ———. *The National Wealth of the United States in the Postwar Period.* Princeton: Princeton University Press for National Bureau of Economic Research, 1962.
[59] ———; Lipsey, Robert E.; and Mendelson, Morris. *Studies in the National Balance Sheet of the United States,* Volumes 1 and 2. Princeton: Princeton University Press for National Bureau of Economic Research, 1963.
[60] ———. *A Study of Saving in the United States, 1955–56,* Volumes I, II and III. Princeton: Princeton University Press, 1956.
[61] ———, assisted by Walter Salant. *The Volume and Components of Saving in the United States, 1933–37.* Studies in Income and Wealth, Volume 3. New York: National Bureau of Economic Research, 1939.
[62] Grebler, Leo; Blank, David M.; and Winnick, Louis. *Capital Formation in Residential Real Estate: Trends and Prospects.* Princeton: Princeton University Press for National Bureau of Economic Research, 1956.
[63] Gurley, John G., and Shaw, E. S. "Financial Aspects of Economic Development." *American Economic Review* (September 1955).
[64] ———. "Financial Intermediaries in the Savings and Investment Process." *Journal of Finance* (May 1956).
[65] ———. *Money in a Theory of Finance.* Washington: Brookings Institution, 1960.
[66] Guttentag, Jack M., and Cagan, Phillip, eds. *Essays on Interest Rates,* Volume 1. New York: National Bureau of Economic Research, 1969.

[67] Haberler, Gottfried. *Consumer Instalment Credit and Economic Fluctuations.* New York: National Bureau of Economic Research, 1942.

[68] Harriss, C. Lowell. *History and Policies of the Home Owner's Loan Corporation.* New York: National Bureau of Economic Research, 1951.

[69] Hickman, W. Braddock. *Corporate Bond Quality and Investor Experience.* Princeton: Princeton University Press for National Bureau of Economic Research, 1958.

[70] ———, assisted by Elizabeth T. Simpson. *Statistical Measures of Corporate Bond Financing since 1900.* Princeton: Princeton University Press for National Bureau of Economic Research, 1960.

[71] ———. "The Term Structure of Interest Rates." Mimeographed. New York: National Bureau of Economic Research, 1942.

[72] ———. *The Volume of Corporate Bond Financing.* New York: National Bureau of Economic Research, 1953.

[73] Hicks, John R. *Value and Capital.* Oxford, England: Clarendon Press, 1939.

[74] Hodgman, Donald R. "Credit, Risk, and Credit Rationing." *Quarterly Journal of Economics* (May 1960), and "Reply." *Quarterly Journal of Economics* (August 1962).

[75] Holland, Daniel M. *Private Pension Funds: Projected Growth.* New York: National Bureau of Economic Research, 1965.

[76] Holthausen, Duncan McC. in collaboration with Malcolm L. Merriam and Rolf Nugent. *The Volume of Consumer Instalment Credit, 1929–1938.* New York: National Bureau of Economic Research, 1940.

[77] Horton, Donald C. *Patterns of Farm Financial Structure.* Princeton: Princeton University Press for National Bureau of Economic Research, 1957.

[78] Houthakker, Hendrik. "Normal Backwardation." In *Value, Capital, and Growth,* edited by J. R. Wolfe. Chicago: Aldine Press, 1968.

[79] Jacoby, Neil H., and Saulnier, Raymond J. *Business Finance and Banking.* New York: National Bureau of Economic Research, 1947.

[80] ———. *Financing Inventory on Field Warehouse Receipts.* New York, National Bureau of Economic Research, 1944.

[81] ———. *Term Lending in Business.* New York: National Bureau of Economic Research, 1942.

[82] Jones, Lawrence A., and Durand, David. *Mortgage Lending Experience in Agriculture.* Princeton: Princeton University Press for National Bureau of Economic Research, 1954.

[83] Juster, F. Thomas, and Shay, Robert P. *Consumer Sensitivity to Finance Rates.* New York: National Bureau of Economic Research, 1964.

[84] Kaysen, Carl. "Industrial and Commercial Debt: A Balance Sheet Analysis." Unpublished manuscript. New York: National Bureau of Economic Research.

[85] Kessel, Reuben A. *The Cyclical Behavior of the Term Structure of Interest Rates.* New York: National Bureau of Economic Research, 1965.

[86] Klaman, Saul B. *The Postwar Résidential Mortgage Market.* New York: National Bureau of Economic Research, 1961.

[87] ———. *The Postwar Rise of Mortgage Companies.* New York: National Bureau of Economic Research, 1959.

[88] ———. *The Volume of Mortgage Debt in the Postwar Decade.* New York: National Bureau of Economic Research, 1958.

[89] Klein, Lawrence R. *Economic Fluctuations in the United States, 1921–41.* New York: John Wiley and Sons, 1950.
[90] Koch, Albert Ralph. *The Financing of Large Corporations, 1920–39.* New York: National Bureau of Economic Research, 1943.
[91] Koopmans, Tjalling C. "Measurement Without Theory." *Review of Economics and Statistics* (August 1947).
[92] Kuznets, Simon, assisted by Elizabeth Jenks. *Capital in the American Economy: Its Formation and Financing.* Princeton: Princeton University Press for National Bureau of Economic Research, 1961.
[93] ———. *The Measurement of National Wealth.* Studies in Income and Wealth, Volume 3. New York: National Bureau of Economic Research, 1938.
[94] Liebenberg, Maurice; Hirsch, Albert A.; and Popkin, Joel, "A Quarterly Econometric Model of the U.S.: A Progress Report," *Survey of Current Business* (May 1966).
[95] Lintner, John. "The Aggregation of Investor's Diverse Judgments and Preferences in Purely Competitive Security Markets." *Journal of Financial and Quantitative Analysis* (December 1969).
[96] ———. "Corporation Finance: Risk and Investment." In *Determinants of Investment Behavior.* Conference of the Universities-National Bureau Committee for Economic Research. New York: National Bureau of Economic Research, 1967.
[97] ———. "Discussion (of Dividends)." *American Economic Review* (May 1964).
[98] ———. "Distribution of Incomes of Corporations Among Dividends, Retained Earnings and Taxes." *American Economic Review* (May 1956).
[99] ———. "The Financing of Corporations." In *The Corporation in Modern Society,* edited by Edward S. Mason. Washington: Howard University Press, 1959.
[100] ———. *Mutual Savings Banks in the Savings and Mortgage Markets.* Boston: Division of Research, Harvard Business School, 1948.
[101] ———. "The Theory of Money and Prices." In *The New Economics,* edited by S. E. Harris. New York: Knopf, 1947.
[102] ———. "The Valuation of Risk Assets and the Selection of Risky Investments in Stock Portfolios and Capital Budgets." *Review of Economics and Statistics* (February 1965).
[103] Lutz, Friedrich A. *Corporate Cash Balances, 1914–43: Manufacturing and Trade.* New York: National Bureau of Economic Research, 1945.
[104] ———. "The Structure of Interest Rates." *Quarterly Journal of Economics* (November 1940).
[105] Macaulay, Frederick R. *Some Theoretical Problems Suggested By Movements of Interest Rates, Bond Yields and Stock Prices in the United States since 1856.* New York: National Bureau of Economic Research, 1938.
[106] Markowitz, Harry. "Portfolio Selection." *Journal of Finance* (March 1952).
[107] ———. *Portfolio Selection.* New York: John Wiley and Sons, 1959.
[108] Meiselman, David, and Shapiro, Eli. *Measurement of Corporate Sources and Uses of Funds.* New York: National Bureau of Economic Research, 1964.
[109] Meiselman, David. *The Term Structure of Interest Rates.* Englewood Cliffs: Prentice-Hall, 1962.

[110] Merwin, Charles L. *Financing Small Corporations in Five Manufacturing Industries, 1926–36*. New York: National Bureau of Economic Research, 1942.
[111] Meyer, John, and Kuh, Edwin. *The Investment Decision*. Cambridge: Harvard University Press, 1957.
[112] Miller, Merton H. "Further Comment on Credit Risk and Credit Rationing." *Quarterly Journal of Economics* (August 1962).
[113] Modigliani, Franco; Rasche, Robert; and Cooper, J. P. "Central Bank Policy, The Money Supply and the Short Term Rate of Interest." Unpublished manuscript. New York: National Bureau of Economic Research.
[114] Modigliani, Franco, and Sutch, Richard. "Innovations in Interest Rate Policy." *American Economic Review* (May 1966).
[115] Moore, Geoffrey H., and Klein, Philip A. *Quality of Consumer Instalment Credit*. New York: National Bureau of Economic Research, 1967.
[116] Morgan, James N. "Goldsmith's Study of United States Saving: A Review Article." *American Economic Review* (June 1956).
[117] Mors, Wallace P. *Consumer Credit Finance Charges: Rate Information and Quotation*. New York: National Bureau of Economic Research, 1965.
[118] Morton, J. E. *Urban Mortgage Lending: Comparative Markets and Experience*. Princeton: Princeton University Press for National Bureau of Economic Research, 1956.
[119] Mossin, Jan. "Equilibrium in a Capital Asset Market." *Econometrica* (October 1966).
[120] ———. "Security Pricing and Investment Criteria in Competitive Markets." *American Economic Review* (December 1969).
[121] Murray, Roger F. *Economic Aspects of Pensions: A Summary Report*. New York: National Bureau of Economic Research, 1968.
[122] Muth, J. F. "Rational Expectation and the Theory of Price Movements." *Econometrica* (July 1961).
[123] National Accounts Review Committee and the National Bureau of Economic Research. *The National Economic Accounts of the United States*. Washington: United States Government Printing Office, 1958.
[124] National Bureau of Economic Research. *The Flow of Funds Approach to Social Accounting*. Studies in Income and Wealth, Volume 26, New York: National Bureau of Economic Research, 1962.
[125] Ott, David J., and Meltzer, Allan H. *Federal Tax Treatment of State and Local Securities*. Washington: Brookings Institution, 1963.
[126] Plummer, Wilbur C., and Young, Ralph A. *Sales Finance Companies and Their Credit Practices*. New York: National Bureau of Economic Research, 1940.
[127] Pogue, G. A. "An Extension of the Markowitz Portfolio Selection Model to Include Variable Transactions, Costs, Short Sales, Leverage Policies, and Taxes." *Journal of Finance* (December 1970).
[128] Pyle, David. "On the Theory of Financial Intermediation." Unpublished thesis. Cambridge: Massachusetts Institute of Technology.
[129] Rasche, R., and Shapiro, H. "The FRB-MIT Econometric Model: Its Special Features." *American Economic Review* (May 1968).
[130] Robinson, Roland I. *Postwar Market for State and Local Government Securities*. Princeton: Princeton University Press for National Bureau of Economic Research, 1960.

[131] Ruggles, Richard. "Methodological Developments." In *Survey of Contemporary Economics,* Volume II, edited by B. F. Haley. Homewood, Illinois: Richard D. Irwin, 1952.

[132] Sametz, Arnold W. "Trends in the Volumes and Composition of Equity Finance." *Journal of Finance* (September 1964).

[133] Saulnier, Raymond J., and Jacoby, Neil H. *Accounts Receivable Financing.* New York: National Bureau of Economic Research, 1943.

[134] Saulnier, Raymond J. *Costs and Returns on Farm Mortgage Lending by Life Insurance Companies, 1945–47.* New York: National Bureau of Economic Research, 1949.

[135] ———; Halcrow, Harold G.; and Jacoby, Neil H. *Federal Lending and Loan Insurance.* Princeton: Princeton University Press for National Bureau of Economic Research, 1958.

[136] ———, and Jacoby, Neil H. *Financing Equipment for Commercial and Industrial Enterprise.* New York: National Bureau of Economic Research, 1944.

[137] ———. *Industrial Banking Companies and Their Credit Practices.* New York: National Bureau of Economic Research, 1940.

[138] ———. *Urban Mortgage Lending by Life Insurance Companies.* New York: National Bureau of Economic Research, 1950.

[139] Seiden, Martin H. *The Quality of Trade Credit.* New York: National Bureau of Economic Research, 1964.

[140] Shapiro, Eli, and White, William L. "Patterns of Business Financing: Some Comments." *Journal of Finance* (December 1965).

[141] Sharpe, William F. "Capital Asset Prices: A Theory of Market Equilibrium Under Conditions of Risk." *Journal of Finance* (September 1964).

[142] Shay, Robert P. *New Automobile Finance Rates, 1924–62.* New York: National Bureau of Economic Research, 1963.

[143] Smith, Keith V. "A Transition Model for Portfolio Revision." *Journal of Finance* (September 1967).

[144] Smyth, D. J. "Saving and the Residual Error." *Bulletin of the Oxford University Institute of Economics and Statistics* (August 1964).

[145] Taylor, Stephen. "Uses of Flow of Funds Accounts in the Federal Reserve System." *Journal of Finance* (May 1963).

[146] Thompson, Lawrence E. "Income Velocity, Liquid Assets of Households and Nonfinancial Corporations, and Monetary Policy." In *Stabilization Policies:* A Research Report of the Commission on Money and Credit. Englewood Cliffs: Prentice-Hall, 1963.

[147] Tinbergen, Jan. *Statistical Testing of Business Cycle Theories,* Volume 2, Geneva: League of Nations, 1939.

[148] Tobin, James, and Brainard, W. "Financial Intermediaries and the Effectiveness of Monetary Policy." *American Economic Review* (May 1963).

[149] Tobin, James. "The Interest-Elasticity of Transactions Demand for Cash." *Review of Economics and Statistics* (August 1956).

[150] ———. "Money and Economic Growth." *Econometrica* (October 1965).

[151] ———. "The Theory of Portfolio Selection." In *The Theory of Interest Rates,* edited by F. H. Hahn and F. P. R. Brechling. London: Macmillan, 1965.

[152] Tostlebe, Alvin S. *Capital in Agriculture: Its Formation and Financing since 1870*. New York: National Bureau of Economic Research, 1957.

[153] Turnovsky, Stephen J. "The Allocation of Corporate Profits Between Dividends and Retained Earnings." *Review of Economics and Statistics* (November 1967.)

[154] Ulmer, Melville J. *Capital in Transportation, Communications and Public Utilities: Its Formation and Financing*. Princeton: Princeton University Press for National Bureau of Economic Research, 1960.

[155] Vining, Rutledge. "Koopmans on the Choice of Variables . . . and . . . Methods of Measurement." *Review of Economics and Statistics* (May 1949).

[156] Wickens, David L. *Residential Real Estate: Its Economic Position*. New York: National Bureau of Economic Research, 1941.

[157] Wojnilower, Albert M. *The Quality of Bank Loans: A Study of Bank Examination Records*. New York: National Bureau of Economic Research, 1962.

[158] Young, Ralph A., and associates. *Personal Finance Companies and Their Credit Practices*. New York: National Bureau of Economic Research, 1940.

[159] Zarnowitz, Victor. *An Appraisal of Short-Term Economic Forecasts*. New York: National Bureau of Economic Research, 1967.

[160] ———; Boschan, Charlotte; and Moore, Geoffrey H. "Business Cycle Analysis of Econometric Model Simulation." In *Econometric Models of Cyclical Behavior*, edited by Bert Hickman. Studies in Income and Wealth, Volume 36. New York: National Bureau of Economic Research, forthcoming.

[161] Zarnowitz, Victor. "Forecasting Economic Conditions: The Record and the Prospect." In *Economic Research: Retrospect and Prospect*. Fiftieth Anniversary Colloquium I. New York: National Bureau of Economic Research, 1972.

DISCUSSION

Includes comments by the chairman, Robert V. Roosa, of Brown Brothers Harriman; and by William J. Baumol, of Princeton University; Sidney Homer, of Salomon Brothers & Hutzler; and James J. O'Leary, of the United States Trust Company of New York, who were the discussants. Remarks made during the open discussion period are not included.

Introductory Remarks by Robert V. Roosa

I know that John Lintner's paper is going to occupy many of you long after these meetings are concluded. You will find that it is more than a remarkable survey of the staggering contribution in space, time, and pagination that the Bureau has contributed to the field of financial research over its lifetime. Not only has he read, digested, criticized, and summarized this vast volume of Bureau contributions, but he has gone on to make suggestions, to point out to the rest of us where he thinks additional Bureau research can go and the changes in dimension and focus that might now be possible on the basis of this massive body of accumulated information and analysis that the Bureau has already provided.

I think I should indicate at the beginning that not only has John Lintner provided splendid coverage of Bureau documentation in the broad area of financial research, he has introduced into his paper the great breadth of knowledge he has in the field as a whole. There are even one or two footnote references to his own contributions which I have always found scintillating and perceptive, and I know you will today in digesting this ambitious paper.

* * *

William J. Baumol: It is a profound privilege to have the opportunity to pay tribute to the National Bureau of Economic Research on the occasion of its fiftieth anniversary and to acknowledge the profession's great debt to it for its contributions to our learning, most notably for leading us to face the quantitative facts, even when we might have been reluctant to do so.

Lintner has performed a substantial task, having undertaken to survey the enormous volume of writings in the field of finance that has over the years been produced under the sponsorship of the Bureau. He has, with his usual thoroughness and insight, produced not only an overview but also a helpful evaluation and a discussion of programs for further research. The validity and comprehensiveness of his discussion suffer from only one disadvantage: They make it very difficult for a discussant who can find little to expand upon and nothing with which to disagree.

I believe Lintner is right in his evaluation of the National Bureau's work in the financial area and right also in the directions to which he points for further research. Though he calls for the use of a theoretical and analytical base, he is careful to avoid the tired discussion of "facts without theory." What makes his observations on this score timely is not primarily a matter of the Bureau's own orientation, but a change in the nature of the theoretical material that is available for use as a framework for empirical research.

For our discipline, the sixties was a decade which brought forth a number of important new ideas. Few of them, however, were contributions to pure theory. Rather, a preponderance of the major innovations were composed of applications of the theory to a number of fields which were formerly the exclusive province of those who provide descriptive and historical materials. For example, the field of public utility regulation, previously devoted heavily to the discussion of legal institutions and the course of their development, has suddenly been inundated by a variety of theoretical writings making heavy use of relatively sophisticated mathematical tools such as Kuhn-Tucker theory. Public finance is another applied field in which the role of formal theory has expanded significantly. In short, it would not be seriously misleading to characterize the ten years that have just passed as the decade of applied theory.

Probably no single field has felt the impact of this development more strongly than that of finance. The rash of literature on the term structure of interest rates does base itself on earlier work by Lutz and Hicks. But recent contributions by writers such as Meiselman and Malkiel have provided a basis and a wealth of hypothesis for systematic empirical research. Modigliani and Miller as well as Professor Lintner have given us a body of materials on the role of dividends and the valuation of stocks which has led to a protracted discussion of fundamental elements in the analysis of financial instruments, and has produced contentions that can only be settled empirically. The portfolio selection analysis contributed by Markowitz and Tobin is still another illustration of this sort of development.

All of this is to say that several decades ago, a call in the field of finance for the empiricists to base their work more heavily on theoretical analysis would not have been easy to heed. Today there seems to be no end to the work of this variety that still needs to be done. Now, therefore, such an admonition is much less an empty gesture because the program of work is there and hardly needs to be laid out.

However, if this is the direction we are now to propose for the work of the Bureau, it would seem that we come a little late. The fact is that many of the outstanding economists associated with the Bureau have already gone off in this direction, and are well along on the way. If one thumbs through the *50th Annual Report* of the National Bureau, one finds described in it a profusion of econometric studies based upon theoretical models, these in a variety of fields. The section devoted to finance is no exception. For example, one finds reported there Cagan's study of the monetary effects of interest rates, Kessel's study of the cyclical behavior of interest rates, Sargent's "Expectations at the Short End of the Yield Curve" and his study of the Gibson paradox,[1] all of them topics clearly having substantial theoretical implications. The fact is that the Bureau's work has already been turned toward theory both as a source for topics for research, and as an area to which its own work can contribute.

This is not meant to imply that the Bureau has abandoned the portions of its work which are devoted to descriptive studies and to data gathering. However, no one would wish for any slackening in the pace of these undertakings. This sort of effort has always produced valuable contributions, and one would hope that it will continue alongside the activities that are more analytical in their orientation.

Let me, in closing, mention one problem in the field of finance not emphasized by Lintner to which one might well ask for the devotion of further research effort. Despite the profusion of developments in the field, both empirical and analytical, the results have so far been fairly disappointing to those who are concerned with application, at least at the micro level. The reason is that so many of the conclusions that have been derived are essentially negative in character. The random walk literature

[1] Phillip Cagan, *The Channels of Monetary Effects on Interest Rates,* forthcoming; Reuben A. Kessel, *The Cyclical Behavior of the Term Structure of Interest Rates,* Occasional Paper 91, 1965; Thomas J. Sargent, "Expectations at the Short End of the Yield Curve: An Application of Macauley's Test," in Jack M. Guttentag, ed., *Essays on Interest Rates,* Vol. II, 1971; and Sargent, "A Study of the Gibson Paradox," *50th Annual Report of the National Bureau of Economic Research,* September 1970.

provides the outstanding illustration, for its implication is that, in the absence of inside information, the attempt to analyze securities and forecast their value may well be a waste of time. Similar in spirit in this respect is Little and Raynor's work indicating that past performance of a company in terms of the rate of growth of its earnings is virtually useless as a predictor of its prospective performance. A group working at Princeton, including Burton G. Malkiel, Richard Quandt, and Peggy Heim has found virtually no relationship between the resources a firm plows back into its capital stock and the rate of growth of its earnings.[2]

All of this has been extremely disquieting to those who have looked to the economists' writings on finance for guidance for their own activities. A bit of debunking is no doubt a good thing, but where does one go from there? All of this is to say that any results which are less negative in character will find a most receptive audience. The field, moreover, does not lack hypotheses, albeit most of them naive. Perhaps the random walk results and the other pieces of evidence mean that there exist in this area no positive results in search of a discoverer, but I think this has not yet been demonstrated. Perhaps someone among those whose work is sponsored by the National Bureau can help to show the way. Certainly, many interesting and challenging issues for research are to be found here.

Sidney Homer: There is only one real answer to the question "What should the National Bureau be doing in the future?" and that is, "Everything." I am sure that John Meyer would add, "If all our subscribers multiply their subscriptions by ten or twenty, we will." I have a little list here today, though, of a few things which would be especially useful from my selfish point of view, some of which are certainly already being worked on. I have in mind more listing of factual data, so that the reader can apply his own theories and perhaps disagree with the author.

Over the years perfectly magnificent work has been done by Raymond Goldsmith and others in flow-of-fund statistics, through the capital market, into and out of various forms of institutions, and all integrated together. At the bottom of the supply list, there is a residual called "miscellaneous and private investors," which in our analyses of

[2] This work almost suggests that companies might as well not plough back any of their funds for all the difference, overall, that it makes to their earnings! The rate of return on new debt seems to be somewhat higher, while the return on new equity turns out, generally, to be significantly more substantial. For the results of this study see William J. Baumol et al., "Earnings Retention, New Capital and the Growth of the Firm," *Review of Economics and Statistics,* November 1970, pp. 345–55.

credit flows we could have pretty well ignored in most of the postwar years. We are now in a period, as you all know, in which "miscellaneous and unaccounted for" are accounting for something like 60 per cent of the capital flows in the bond market. I have over the last few years been needling anyone who is available to be needled—the FED, the SEC, and the National Bureau—to look into this massive supply-of-credit field, which last year bought over $25 billion of bonds net, and to break it down into component parts that have some meaning, so that the flows can be traced insofar as possible from savings institutions, stocks, and so on into bonds; so that we may know something about this group—as much as we know about savings banks, for example, and life insurance companies.

Second would be further analysis of the government sector. Not enough has been done on the role of government in our capital markets. The proportion attributed to government in the GNP analysis I suspect strongly underestimates the role of government in our economy. More and more in our capital markets, the device of guaranteeing private obligations is becoming massive, and with tremendous implications for the future. I would suggest this be studied on a broader base than the GNP base, particularly as regards its effects on the capital market, its effects on the economy, and its effects on the distribution of resources.

Next, I would suggest a very lively topic which will not come as a surprise to most of you: the topic of the role of social priorities in the capital markets, the question of how resources are directed by pure open-market rationing as distinguished from national objectives and national priorities. It seems to me that this is not new but of greatly expanding importance, and I haven't seen it really covered in a complete way.

We have another topic that has become very lively this year, the question of liquidity: the quality of institutional portfolios, the liquidity of institutions, and the liquidity of industrial firms. We know this is not purely a statistical matter; so far as I know there is no set of ratios that answers the question, because liquidity is at least 50 per cent psychological.

But the whole liquidity question and the credit question and the credit quality question are vital. I do not know how the econometricians work it into their models. One week the lending policies of American institutions are among the most liberal in years; a week later, they are among the most conservative in years. Something has happened—I'm referring now to the Penn Central, but this is only a symbol—there are plenty of other situations that have worried lending officers. If their credit policies change, money flows change, and there is a vital effect on the economy. No doubt in a broad sense this has been studied, but I would think that in a specific and practical sense it would be a big field for research work now.

That is far from the end of my list, but those are the high spots. I will stop here and make two general observations. A great many important statistical studies have been done, by the National Bureau and by others, that are extremely useful. It is regrettable that in many cases when they come out the latest statistics in them are four years old. I know this is a mechanical problem that is extremely difficult to solve, but the pertinence of the document is greatly impaired. Along the same lines, and again from my practical standpoint, I would like to see a great deal of the statistical work brought up to date. I know it is the policy of the Bureau to do the basic work in the hope that some government agency will keep it up to date. In the case of flow of funds this has been done, but there are other instances where this has not been done. I would personally find very useful some periodic publication that brings past statistical studies up to date, at least that type of study that can be brought up to date in a ready manner, so that the study becomes fresh all of a sudden, and useful.

James O'Leary: When I read John Lintner's paper I had the same feeling that Bill Baumol had. Lintner has done a monumental job. The books he has reviewed would occupy about twenty feet of shelving in any library. In effect, what he has done is a one-man exploratory committee job on what's going on in the financial research field and what needs to be done. I think the Bureau, which in the past has had exploratory committees, owes a big debt of gratitude to John Lintner for the job he has done.

As I read through that paper, I was a little taken aback because I hadn't realized quite what the nature of the paper would be. I expected this to be a paper oriented toward monetary issues. As I got into it, I kept meeting old friends all along the way, and it was a very heartwarming experience for me. I had the great fortune right after World War II when teaching at Duke to be offered the job of director of investment research for the Life Insurance Association of America. One part of my job was to help the life insurance business decide on financial research that it felt it could support.

In the period from 1947 through 1967, while I was involved in this, we advanced something like two million dollars in research funds to the National Bureau. I suppose today, in terms of what that will buy in research, it would be equivalent to maybe four or five million dollars in research funds. We got involved in this actually before I was on the scene in the very early projects that are described in John's paper where the original exploratory committee of the Bureau in 1937 came up with some projects. We were participants, for example, in the corporate bond project that Brad Hickman carried out. As you look through this list we did the financing of Ray Goldsmith's study of savings. It was one of the most exciting two years of my life to be closely associated with this, not actually in a research role but very closely associated with it. And that wasn't done, incidentally, as a National Bureau project. It was done under R. W. Goldsmith Associates, before Goldsmith became associated with the Bureau. The interesting thing there was that we clothed him with an advisory committee so that he'd be completely independent. That advisory committee had some notable names on it. It had, among the economists, Win Riefler as chairman. It also had on it Jack Viner of Princeton, Sumner Slichter of Harvard, Arthur F. Burns, Simon Kuznets, and Ted Yntema. In addition we financed another project called the Study of the Postwar Capital Markets, exploring the changes in the capital market. There were a number of participants in this. This is the project in which Saul Klaman did his great job on the residential mortgage market; and Roland Robinson, a great job on state and local government financing. Then we financed Kuznets's study of capital requirements. Incidentally, in many of these cases, the idea of the projects actually originated with the life insurance people. We financed a study of interest rates which the Bureau has done. Phil Cagan had a very important part in that. As I mentioned, we financed Hickman's corporate bond project and many others. We put money into the pension fund study conducted by Roger Murray. So I take a great deal of pride when I hear John talk about what has come out of this research; I agree with him. I think it has been a very, very important contribution, and a great deal is owed some of the men who helped obtain the financing of these projects—in particular, John Sinclair, who later headed the National Industrial Conference Board; F. W. Ecker, who later became the chief executive of Metropolitan Life; Don Slichter, president of Northwestern Mutual; George Conklin, president of the Guardian Life Company; and Robert B. Patrick, senior vice president of Bankers Life of Iowa.

I think we have to do more to get the commercial banks and other financial institutions interested in this sort of approach. As I see it, the amount of money that has to go into financial research, if it is to be effective with the Bureau and other places, is a large multiple of what's been done in the past.

Now let me just wind up by saying, I couldn't agree more with John Lintner's suggestions as to the direction that research should take. I think it is true that no revolutionary change is needed. The kind of research that the Bureau has proved itself so well in is what it should continue to do. I agree there should be some change in strategy in the direction of more analytical work rather than purely a collection of figures. But it will be awfully hard for the Bureau to do this because the financial system is changing so quickly that simply the gathering of data is going to continue to be a major part of this whole picture. I think the sort of issucs and problems John has raised are right, and all I would like to do is to add one or two that occur to me. There is one big one, and then there are others that are more obvious. The big one is this: Since the latter part of 1965 there has been an escalation of inflation, and along with it there has been the sharp rise in interest rates, with interest rates now at record high levels. The likelihood is that interest rates, even though they will fluctuate cyclically, are going to continue to remain at high levels. What I would like to see the Bureau do is to study the question of how our financial system is affected by this sort of condition; how it is affected by Federal Reserve policies now as compared with a condition in which we had a lower level of interest rates and more in the way of price stability. I think that there are profound effects on the financial institutions if you analyze them in these terms. For example, how is this sort of condition affecting the cash flow of the financial institutions? How is it affecting their willingness and their ability to make forward investment commitments to buy bonds and mortgages? How is it affecting their preference for equities or equity kickers? How does monetary policy work differently today under these sets of conditions than would have been the case, say, even three or four years ago, or certainly ten years ago? If we should go through another cycle such as the one we had in 1966, or in 1969–70, I wonder whether some of our financial institutions could survive. I think that some are more threatened than others. Can our financial system as we have known it in the past continue to function successfully with a 4 per cent rate of inflation, which is what many people are assuming?

To take a few other areas, perhaps the Bureau could do more in the way of putting some meat and bones on the whole question of how expectation of inflation affects investment decisions. This is a tremendously important development. I don't see quite how the Bureau can get at it in a quantitative way, but, I think, through close contact with decision-makers in the financial markets, perhaps an awful lot can be done to help get a better understanding of the effects of the expectation of inflation on the bond and stock markets. Our financial system is changing rapidly. As you look at the catalogue of what the Bureau has done, you can see how far out of date it is in terms of what's going on today. For example, there is very little that the Bureau has done in the area of at least updating information on mortgage loans on income-type property. Very little in the way of data has been collected on the whole use of equity kickers on loans. I would say, finally, I think there is a great opportunity now to make another advance in the flow-of-funds area to get gross figures. The flow-of-funds data are still just net changes in outstandings, whereas, for example, in the life insurance business, there is now a rich body of data on the gross cash flow for investment. I think this sort of data probably is available in some of the other financial institutions as well.

* * *

Closing Remarks by Roosa

It does seem to me that we have assembled a list here which is largely action oriented in terms of the implications of the array of suggestions for future research. I think this is in keeping with the approach that John Lintner has taken in his paper, indicating that broadly speaking so much has been done in describing the what of the financial system that we need now more on the interrelations and the why. All the same, I think we must agree with Jim O'Leary and Sidney Homer that much of the work that has already been done by the Bureau that stands as classic is still in need of updating—of continuous testing against new data. There does have to be a compromise between these two kinds of objectives, and I am sure will always continue to be. I'd like to sum up what I think are several of the action-oriented suggestions that have been made thus far, and then add a couple.

It does seem to me that John has indicated the need for getting inside the boxes of the whole flow-of-funds analysis, for updating and digging further into the Goldsmith and the Kuznets work, not merely in terms of the data, vast as that is, but in terms of the causation. In addition, we have had some variants on that fundamental approach in Bill Baumol's recognition that the Bureau in its effort to move in new directions has had, as I think he put it, an increasing infusion of mathematical inspiration. I may not have accurately paraphrased him, but the implications there, in terms of the techniques of data manipulation and in developing the power of theoretical analysis, are clear enough. But he took this in another direction as well. He was a little mystified, if I am not unduly generalizing from his more precise statement, as to how the capital allocation mechanism really works and how it can be considered rational as it relates to the application of retained earnings in the total process of capital formation in the economy. He can't also quite understand how the returns that he finds on new equity and on the commitment of new investment funds in the established large and growing corporations explain the claim in relative terms that they are exerting on the total of our supply of available savings—the contribution to the capital stock that they do in fact carry through. I may be sharpening too invidiously what he said much more delicately, and I may have misunderstood. But I would suggest that this is one set of implications that probably does deserve additional thought and consideration.

Before we get too far with those, we have to come to one of the several suggestions that Sidney Homer made, because we are entering what probably is another mutation phase in the array of criteria that society is going to accept or impose on itself. Implications of this for the processes of capital allocation have yet to be determined. The point Sidney made was that we haven't yet figured it out, although some of us find that we are harassed or buffeted or moved or pressed every day or so by the criticism we are receiving that social priorities are not adequately represented in the processes of capital allocation. We have to find a clearer way of expressing what they are and how they can be quantified, how they can be represented in the investment process. I think to be more specific, Sidney also reminded us that the miscellaneous categories in some of our financial data have now become so large that we lack an explanation of the principal sources of investment in fixed-interest obligations which we can't penetrate further. Of course, we aren't going to get the answer satisfactorily there.

In addition, if we are going to find not only the who but the why, we must go on into some of the other questions that he and Jim O'Leary raised. The question, of course, that is going to have a pervasive significance, as long as any of us remember those two words Penn Central, is the significance of liquidity not merely for the financial institutions but for the industrial firm. What does it mean and how are we usefully going to establish standards, both of evaluation and performance, that will fit with the criteria we want to have for rational capital allocation in the system? All of this can become almost revolutionarily terrifying if we let ourselves think too far. The implications in pure research are, I think, themselves sufficiently challenging. As Jim O'Leary brought us closer to the present day in another respect, he stressed that none of us really have satisfactorily thought through yet, as far as I know, even the purely abstract systematic implications of our kind of economy, operating in an environment in which it must be assumed that there will be a continuing pattern of inflation—I think he said at the 4 per cent level. We haven't really thought through what that kind of outside given element will do to so much of the pattern of interrelations that we would otherwise be measuring from past performance. Just within the past two years we've had a mutation or followed a path that won't be completely reversible, even if we do get lower rates of inflation in the future.

The significance of having had this bath of inflation—whether or not it continues—is certainly an area we want to be certain is explored and reflected in the many more detailed and specific projects that the Bureau will be carrying forward. As he said in concluding, and this is implied in many of the other things I've also mentioned, there is the more specific translation of this inflation mentality into expectations as they affect investment decisions, that is, the investment decisions of the firm as well as the commitment of the lender or the source of funds.

In all this we may have passed through a period that is so rich in new experience that we can well justify spending a major part of any research effort such as that of the Bureau in trying not to look at the longer time series that will, perhaps, over the decades ahead provide the more lasting evidences of the inner patterns of the economy. We may find that we are going to need and want to devote more attention to the study of the special phenomena that came with this, let's hope, short-lived experience of rapid inflation in this kind of economy. It is quite understandable and, I think, all of us have shared a bit of it, that during an inflation of this kind there should have been a revival of that search for the Holy Grail or the simple formula that always characterizes mankind in the face of crisis or new challenge. This time, we called back to Chicago and came out with the revival of the monetarist approach, which is probably likely to shift back into a position of more balanced perspective than might have been implied in some of the things that were receiving widespread attention a year or so ago. Nonetheless, I think, what we are going to want to do is to study it in every way we can. This will involve the selective study of cases, as well as the analysis of data, and the extent to which, in this recent period when inflation has been the dominant characteristic of our economic performance, the monetary phenomenon as such has attained a special new significance and a new force, a force certainly greater than would have been attributed to it, as John Lintner points out in his paper, in any of the earlier model building. In this respect, he does go back as early as the first Klein models twenty years ago, indicating (in keeping with our Keynesian biases of those days) that very little recognition was then given to money as an independent influence.

Reaching outside this need for bringing up to date in the present context what deserves to survive of the monetarist view, there is another area of financial analysis which no one has mentioned today. It is a part of the Bureau's effort nonetheless, and since I am generally considered to be rather fanatic on this subject, I wouldn't dare turn the meeting over to you without mentioning it: We have had new developments in the balance-of-payments relations of this country and in the rest of the world as well.

Another new phenomenon to which the Bureau has already given some attention (as have members of the Bureau staff on their own) is the phenomenon of the Eurodollar market, both short and long. The relations between the supply of and demand for funds in that market inject another dimension of altogether different scale in magnitude and in implications for the conduct of our financial markets, an altogether different dimension from anything that existed during the period when most of the data to which John refers in his paper were being put together. I think we have here another important area, and not merely for debunking the significance of what I suppose this year will be an official settlements deficit of eight or nine billion dollars that will occur largely because a completely extraterritorial volume of forty billion odd dollars can move back and forth between private holders abroad and central banks abroad, and such movement happens to be defined as a deficit in the U.S. balance of payments. These are new phenomena, but these patterns of movement have their ricochets, with implications reaching back into the money market, and to some extent into the bond market, sometimes as a safety valve and sometimes as a source of new fear and concern, which I'm sure somewhere in this scale of projects deserves some mention.

I will close with one more comment. I have been a little struck, and I am not sure whether this is too naive to mention, but I'm a little struck with the alacrity with which the present Administration has adopted an approach that some of us like to be identified with from an earlier Administration; that is, the concept of the economy's potential as a guide both to fiscal policy and to the potential risks of inflation. My own thought, when we were giving a lot of attention in 1960–62 to this same concept (beginning from a low level of employment), was that if this potential were to be usable as the base on which to fill out additional spending—either through a government deficit or an easier monetary policy—it required a little more than just simply projecting a 4 per cent line across a piece of graph paper. There was also going to have to be an underlying capital base—a capital base which would be expanding, improving, or enlarging, or raising the productive quotient of the total mix of men and labor in the economy. Conversely, if we were to assume stagnation in the capital formation process, we wouldn't be able to draw that handsome line across the graph paper. What I suggest is, at least as I saw it in those days, we couldn't really draw that line unless we had also assured ourselves of a fairly sustained pattern of capital formation in the direction of intensifying the capital structure.

That's why, at least in my view, we began so aggressively and succeeded only after two years in introducing the investment credit as a part of this procedure. Whether or not you like that technique, it is a good one to study—for its effects as well. Every time people in my firm or other's write a story about any firm they are considering investing in these days, three or four lines have to be inserted about how, without the investment credit, this had happened or that had happened. People were inclined to say, and people in high places said a year or so ago, that the investment credit was a mere fiction, but the analysis of the individual cases now is certainly showing that, at least in those that I see, and there are quite a few, the elimination of the investment credit is doing something to impair the capital market. It is possible that here in the Bureau's action-oriented part of the program there may be something worth exploring; that is, whether we can safely assume that this projection of the full employment potential for the economy can exist regardless of what is going on or permitted or encouraged insofar as capital formation is concerned.